Award-Winning

QUILTS

& Their Makers

Vol. I: The Best of American Quilter's Society Shows
1985-1987

Edited by Victoria Faoro

American Quilter's Society
P.O. Box 3290   Paducah, KY 42002-3290

Library of Congress Cataloging-in-Publication Data

Faoro, Victoria.
Award-winning quilts & their makers/edited by Victoria Faoro.
p. cm.
Includes index.
Contents: v.1. The best of American Quilter's Society shows, 1985-1987.
ISBN 0-89145-972-3: $24.95
1. Quilts–United States–Awards. 2. Quiltmakers–United States–Biography. 3. Quilts–Awards.
I. American Quilter's Society. II. Title: Award-winning quilts and their makers.
III. Title: Quilts & their makers.
NK9112.F36 1991 746.9'7'097309048–dc20 91-11758 CIP

Additional copies of this book may be ordered from: American Quilter's Society
P.O. Box 3290, Paducah, KY 42002-3290 @$24.95. Add $1.00 for postage & handling.
10 9 8 7 6 5 4 3 2 1

ACKNOWLEDGMENTS

AQS thanks all of the quiltmakers for giving graciously of their time to respond to questions, for furnishing photographs of themselves and for giving permission to include photographs of their quilts.

AQS also thanks all members of AQS and everyone participating in AQS Shows – those who have entered quilts, volunteered, attended. Without you, the show and this book would not be possible.

AQS also thanks quiltmakers everywhere, who continue to produce the exciting work that first made us want to become involved.

TABLE OF CONTENTS

INTRODUCTION

In 1984 Meredith and Bill Schroeder launched a drive to build an organization
dedicated to promoting the accomplishments of the American quilter.
Their goals were to develop a membership organization, publish a quarterly
magazine for members, hold a national quilt show with meaningful monetary
awards and build a national headquarters and museum to honor today's
quiltmakers.

The American Quilter's Society was the result, along with its magazine *American
Quilter*, its annual Quilt Show and Contest, and its new Museum of the American
Quilter's Society.

This book, Vol. I, documents the first three years of the AQS Quilt Show and
Contest, 1985-87. But even more so, it documents today's outstanding quiltmakers,
the people to whom the American Quilter's Society is dedicated.

There is a great range of styles, techniques, and visions in the quilts that won
awards those three years, just as there is a great range in the people
who made them. In preparing this book, we contacted the quiltmakers involved
so their current thoughts could be included, to give a sense of the role that
quiltmaking, quilt competitions, and these particular awards have played
in their lives.

AQS is delighted to be able to once again present this outstanding collection of
quilts and quilters – and looks forward to sharing more award winners in upcoming
volumes. AQS also thanks all of the quiltmakers and quilt lovers who have
continued to make each AQS show an even more exciting event.

Quilt Show & Contest

1985

The first American Quilter's Society Quilt Show & Contest was held April 26-28, 1985, at the Executive Inn Riverfront in Paducah, Kentucky.

Judges for quilt awards were Patricia Morris, Glassboro, NJ; Katy Christopherson, Louisville, KY; and Maria McCormick-Snyder, Cazenovia, NY. Awards sponsored by the American Quilter's Society were made in the following categories:

Patchwork, Amateur
Applique, Amateur
Other Techniques, Amateur
Wall Quilt, Amateur
Group/Team

Patchwork, Professional
Applique, Professional
Other Techniques, Professional
Wall Quilt, Professional

In each category three awards were made: 1st place, $750; 2nd place, $500; 3rd place, $300.

Two additional overall awards were also given: the Gingher Award for Excellence of Workmanship, a $1,000 award sponsored by Gingher, Inc., and the AQS Best of Show Award, a $10,000 award.

The exhibit included 409 quilts representing 46 states, Canada and Japan. During the show, many of the 7,750 people who attended voted for their favorite quilt, and a Viewer's Choice award was later made.

A display of antique quilts and a 24-merchant shoppers' mall completed this first annual show for quilters and quilt lovers.

Katherine E. Inman
Athens, Ohio

Oriental Fantasy

This original Oriental-style design was the result of Katherine Inman's having lived for two years in Southeast Asia. She says of its development, "One night was spent with paper and crayons at the kitchen table. By morning, the design was finalized down to the last detail." Popular with judges and viewers alike, this quilt has won numerous awards

best of show

1985 AQS Show & Contest

in many shows and competitions.

The quilt is entirely made of 100% cotton fabrics. About the quilting and embroidery, Katherine says, "The Chinese symbols quilted in blue were from my imagination, and have no meaning that I am aware of. The outside border quilting is bamboo with Chinese temples in each corner, and the patch of embroidery in center panel is my name in Chinese."

When asked about her award, Katherine says, "Just having a quilt accepted for the AQS show is a great reward in itself. Seeing all the marvelous quilts in competition makes one feel humble indeed. Meeting quilters, and making many new friends has been a very positive result of the show." She continues, "Before, the guilt I felt when I sewed in the daytime was a big problem for me. As a result, I stitched most of this quilt at night – quite often sewing all night. Now I can devote an entire day to a project with no guilt whatsoever. It's great!"

She adds that not only does she now spend much time quilting, but she also works in "...a large wonderful room with three windows and two skylights. The work table in the center is so big it had to be taken apart to get it into the house."

Hesitant to give advice to others, Katherine simply says, "...in my own case I never pause in ripping out stitching which I feel could be improved upon. For me that is not time wasted." She continues, "The one thing I can urge quilters to do, however, is by all means enter shows. That is the most

"The objective was to make a quilt that would have a quiet and peaceful effect in the room. My hope is that this was accomplished."

ORIENTAL
FANTASY
82" x 98"
1985
Katherine E.
Inman

Museum of AQS
Collection

effective way to compare your work with others. We certainly can't be winners every time, but it is a great learning experience, and next year it just may be your turn to win."

In looking back at this quilt, Katherine is still pleased, but thinks that if she could do it over, she "might do a better job!"

Dorothy Finley
Memphis, Tennessee

Dot's Vintage 1983

When asked about her involvement in quilting, Dorothy Finley explains, "My interest in quilts started in 1974 when my husband Irby came in from work one afternoon with an armload of quilt books for me to look at. (Illness had forced me to give up working, and he told me he didn't need any more handknit sweaters.) So, just to please him, I started

gingher award

for workmanship
1985 AQS Show & Contest

thumbing through these books and soon found myself stopping here and there to read a bit. Before long I was completely fascinated with the history and folklore of some of the old quilt patterns and decided I would make one quilt."

Dorothy has since completed 34! She comments, "The old, historical patterns are the ones I like to make using today's pretty fabrics,

and as I sit and work I often wonder how our grandmothers would have liked to have had our beautiful, bright fabrics in their scrapbags. I'm building a collection of future heirlooms. I want to continue making the old, old patterns with lots of quilting on each. I like to search for the old quilting motifs, bring them out of hiding between the pages of a book, and use them on my quilts so that this generation and future generations can see and appreciate the motifs and designs used by our ancestors....Needless to say, I'm completely hooked on quilt-

making and usually spend several hours on it each day."

She says this very complex, original-design medallion quilt was actually inspired by a tiny piece of purple polished cotton fabric. With its appliqued and stuffed grapes, bows, and bands; quilted and stuffed channels; and quilted antique motifs; it is an astounding accomplishment. In addition to winning this AQS award, the quilt was also granted "Masterpiece" status by the National Quilting Association and earned Dorothy her Master's Certification, making her the second NQA member to achieve this status.

In the tradition of quiltmakers of the past, Dorothy deliberately omitted a quilted grape from one of the bunches of grapes in the top right panel of this quilt. "A bird ate the missing grape" can be found embroidered on the back of the quilt.

Dorothy's advice to quiltmakers: "Always do your very best."

Dorothy spent 2,265 hours making DOT'S VINTAGE. It was totally handmade, and its quilting involved 8,500 feet of quilting thread.

DOT'S VINTAGE
1983
84" x 100"
1983
Dorothy Finley

Museum of AQS Collection

Marcia J. Lutz
Ball Ground, Georgia

If The Amish Did Deco

In developing the original design for this quilt Marcia J. Lutz used ideas from an Art Deco stained-glass design book. The colors were inspired by a grass-green, red-orange and purple Tiffany lamp she had seen in an antique shop.

Hand-pieced, hand-quilted, and made of 100% cotton fabrics, the quilt took about 1,000 hours to com-

first place

1985 AQS Show & Contest Patchwork, Amateur

plete. Marcia says that she constructed the quilt by drawing the design on paper, tracing the pattern pieces using a light box, adding the seam allowances, and then sewing the pieces together.

Speaking of the development of the design, Marcia says, "My son Cliff arranged the four center blocks while we were on vacation in Florida. He asked if he could 'play' with them; then, the quilt grew out from there. The 'ray' blocks are mirror images. The quilting on these mirror images was done with 18 pattern pieces in order to maintain consistency with the zig-zag quilting pattern."

About her background, Marcia says, "I was raised on a farm near Pendleton, Indiana. I attended John Herron Art Institute in Indianapolis,

and later moved to Seattle, Washington, where I worked at the University of Washington and attended art classes. In 1974, I married and moved to the Atlanta, Georgia, area. Presently, I reside in Ball Ground, Georgia, and work part time at a quilt shop in Roswell, Georgia."

"Because I was a winner at AQS, I feel I've been invited to exhibit my quilts at other national shows from Stone Ridge, New York, to the West Coast Quilter's Conference in Sacramento, CA. I've felt proud to know something I enjoy doing measures up in competition, and it pleases me to know others have enjoyed seeing my quilts in shows."

"Allow your inner voice to come through – don't be resistant to trying an innovative idea. Be willing to do what it takes. Sometimes I felt I spent many long hours quilting instead of spending them with my family in activities. But, in order to see my ideas through to completion, I made the choice to spend these hours quilting."

IF THE AMISH
DID DECO
83" x 83"
1985
Marcia J. Lutz

Arnold H. Savage
Avon, Ohio

Opus 31; Numbers 24:17

Arnold was sitting in church "in the merry, merry month of May," when the Pastor directed him to the lesson of the sermon for that day: Numbers, Chapter 24, Verse 17. There he saw, "And out of Jacob shall come a STAR!" and much to his surprise, there in church began his original design for this award-winning quilt.

Solid-colored cotton fab-

second place

1985 AQS Show & Contest Patchwork, Amateur

rics, a cotton batt and 3½ spools of cotton quilting thread (225 yards per spool!) went into its making, and strip piecing methods were used for the construction. Arnold says he quilted freehand – with no design marked – and on his lap without basting stitches or a frame securing the layers. The quilting design's straight lines move through all parts of the star center and radiate out.

He says of the quilt, "I like it even more each day that I see it and am amazed that it came out of me." In speaking of the Amish influence on his work, he comments, "I have been quilting for 55 years. In doing research on my family the past few years, I found that we were descended from the Amish. A great-great-grand uncle was the first Amish Bishop in Ohio (Holmes

County). My relatives left the Amish during a great Schism that rocked the faith in the 1850's. No wonder I have such a great feel for those wonderful Amish quilts!"

Arnold reports that winning this award in the AQS contest made him "...a much better quilter and much more eager to design a contemporary piece as well as accept more readily the work present-day quiltists are doing."

His advice to other quiltmakers: "Perfect your skills to a high level of competence if you expect to enter a competition, and please get a 'feel' for the contest before you attempt to enter a work. Also be very careful that you submit clear, sharp slides that do justice to your work. It is best to hang your work on a plain wall without any people holding it or without any distracting "props" in the picture. Take as many as 10 different snaps of the quilt with 10 different settings and use the best one."

Numbers 24:17:

I see him, but not now; I behold him, but not nigh:
a star shall come forth out of Jacob, and a scepter shall rise out of Israel;
it shall crush the forehead of Moab, and break down all the sons of Sheth.

OPUS 31;
NUMBERS 24:17
72" x 80"
©1985
Arnold H. Savage

Pat Abbott
New Berlin, Illinois

Topsy

Speaking of making TOPSY, Pat Abbott says, "I was a total novice when I began. I had taken beginning classes – that was all – when I saw the Jinny Beyer fabrics (not little calicos). I had to do something with them. The colors were marvelous. I just began." She adds, "It is totally constructed by hand. At that time I knew nothing of machine piecing, which I do

third place

1985 AQS Show & Contest Patchwork, Amateur

more of now. The quilting designs just developed as I worked."

Pat says she had much encouragement from family and friends as she developed this quilt. She explains, "It took me almost a year to complete, and had I not had all the support, it might have been laid aside. So between personal motivation and support, anything can be accomplished." Looking at the quilt now, she comments, "I see so much that could be improved, especially some of the quilting, but I still love it.

The design, color, fabrics are still pleasing to me and my family loves it."

Pat discusses her background: "I have done most kinds of needlework since I was a child – knitting, embroidery, crewel, needlepoint (lots of needlepoint), clothing, everything but crochet – and no quilting, which I had always loved and greatly admired, but just never done. My husband and I have been married 43 years have three grown children, five grandchildren, taught elementary school 20 years, worked retail, traveled a little (not enough), played golf a little; I have a good and busy life. After winning *two* awards at the first AQS show, which was my thrill of a life-

time, I bought a quilt shop in Springfield, IL. Owning a quilt shop has been an exciting and wonderful experience."

Speaking of her award she comments, "Had I not made TOPSY and won, I'd still be going to any quilt show I could. I'd still be admiring beautiful quilts, but winning has led to becoming a quilt shop owner, has broadened my appreciation of new and innovative techniques, has introduced me to a world of creative and talented quilters – and has given me the tools with which to, when I have time, put together interesting and soul-satisfying quilts!"

She advises other quiltmakers: "Go for it – believe in yourself and what you are doing."

"Owning a quilt shop has been lots of hard work and has left very little time for my own projects, but the people I have met have made it all worthwhile. Quilters are special."

TOPSY
108" x 120"
1985
Pat Abbott

TOPSY also won the First Quilt Award at the 1985 show.

Doreen Speckmann
Madison, Wisconsin

The Blade

Doreen Speckmann says, "I guess I am attracted to quilt design and tend to describe the ones I make in terms of their design instead of the colors." THE BLADE was the fourth quilt Doreen made with her original block,

first place

*1985 AQS Show & Contest
Patchwork, Professional*

Wingra Star. She says, "I loved the block but the first two pieces were flops. For color, I wanted to see the effect of background value changes." Asked what she would like people to know about this quilt, she says, "I would like people to know that I have never been comfortable with the colors. They have always seemed cold and hard. I much prefer working with prints now." About the quilt she adds, "I feel detached from it. When I look at the pictures, I wish I had put a border on it."

Doreen began quilting in 1977 after years of knitting and needlework. She taught quiltmaking in Madison for years before "going on the road."

Asked about her AQS award she comments, "I think the biggest effect winning an award has had on my quilt-making is to validate my work. When I work on a quilt, I get so close to it that I sometimes lose perspective. I get caught up in what is wrong with the quilt – how the stitches could have been smaller, the piecing even more perfect. Having a quilt judged and having it win puts all that out of my mind. The end result is that I am much more forgiving with my work and now enjoy the process even more than I did before."

Her advice to other quilt-

makers: "On the subject of competitions and quilt shows in general, I realized a long time ago when going to quilt shows how much I appreciated others for entering their quilts so I could enjoy them. It only seemed right to pay back by entering my quilts as soon as they were presentable. Entering a competition was just the next step. Knowing that other quiltmakers would be looking at my work inspired me to work harder. What might have been good enough for my bedroom wasn't good enough for another quilter. So I fine tuned my skills — bias binding with mitered corners, more-than-adequate quilting, ect. When these skills came as second nature, I could have more fun with the designs and color. My advice to other quiltmakers is to learn your craft and then have fun. Make quilts with conviction, play with color, do the unexpected, and enter quilt shows."

"The Wingra Star block I used in THE BLADE was created by laying a Swamp Patch over a Peaky and Spike with Ice Cream Cones block. It fascinated me to see what happened when I laid one block over the other."

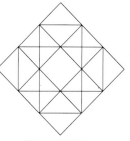

SWAMP PATCH

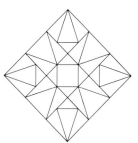

PEAKY AND SPIKE WITH
ICE CREAM CONES

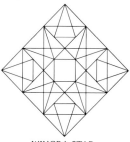

WINGRA STAR

THE BLADE
62" x 84"
©1985
Doreen
Speckmann

Museum of AQS Collection

Imogene Gooch
Rockville, Indiana

Feathered Star Sampler

Speaking of making this quilt, Imogene Gooch says, "All my piecing and quilting is done by hand. I used nine different blocks. These were placed inside a Feathered Star, making the total block 24" x 24". Prairie Points were added around the border."

Continuing, Imogene adds, "This quilt was made for the Indianapolis Blocks and Star contest in 1983. I was influenced by Jinny Beyer's work

second place

*1985 AQS Show & Contest
Patchwork, Professional*

with print stripes. I used all Jinny Beyer fabric; it was a challenge to see the many different designs that could be made. The quilt placed 7th in the contest; the judges felt that because I had used all Jinny Beyer border prints, I had not used my own coordinating ability, but thank goodness all judges don't agree."

"I started quilting with my mother when I was very young, because she felt I should learn, and made me do it. At that time I was not all that enthused. It was not until she had passed away and I was confined at home after back surgery that I thought about using up the scraps that had been left from her quilts, that I became interested in piecing and designing. I found such contentment, and a feeling that I was not wasting my time (like reading or watching television). I picked up a few quilt books, attended a few quilt shows, and was hooked for life. Because of more back problems, I have not been able to attend quilt shows lately, but I sure hope to be able to come to the

Museum of the American Quilter's Society."

Imogene's FEATHERED STAR SAMPLER which was meant to be given to her granddaughter, Elizabeth, who was born during the time the quilt was being made, was purchased in 1985 for the Museum of the American Quilter's Society. Imogene says, "After the quilt was finished, I was very pleased with it. I had spent many hours designing it and I always feel each quilt I make is a part of me. I guess I still have the same feeling about it; it's almost like I have lost a very dear friend. Though I don't have the quilt around where I can see it every day, I am very happy and proud it will be in the AQS museum, where it will be well taken care of and enjoyed by others. After winning in the Paducah contest, I made another FEATHERED STAR SAMPLER for my granddaughter, identical to the first one."

"I came home from the AQS show and almost immediately begin to make my second FEATHERED STAR SAMPLER for the Stearns and Foster contest. It was chosen to

"I used nine different blocks: Mexican Star, French Star, Rolling Star, Maltese Star, Falling Star, 8-pointed (Lemon) Star, Blazing Star, LeMoyne Star, and Morning Star."

FEATHERED
STAR SAMPLER
110" x 110"
1983
Imogene Gooch

Museum of AQS Collection

go to Houston out of 452 quilts. My sister and I decided to go to the show, and much to my amazement it placed fifth. I entered the next S&F show with *Tulip Bowl* and received honorable mention and won a Caribbean cruise for two. It was a wonderful trip and I'm sure one we would never have taken had it not been for my quilting."

Asked to give advice to other quiltmakers, Imogene says, "Having taught many quilt classes, I have come to the conclusion that it takes a very determined type of person to stay with it until they can master the piecing and quilting. If they have the patience, determination and like competition, I say 'GO FOR IT.'"

Annabel Baugher
Galt, Missouri

Winter Star Medallion

Speaking of her background, Annabel says, "I am a farmer's daughter and a farmer's wife. I did not grow up in a family of quilters, but a family who appreciated and practiced excellent hand sewing. My first real quilting experience came in 1973 when our daughter-in-law asked me to make her a quilted bedspread. My quilts are designed with the bed in a beautiful bedroom in mind."

third place

1985 AQS Show & Contest Patchwork, Professional

She continues, "Since my quilts are made with the idea they will be used, touched and yes, washed, fabrics are chosen that will hold up well in these conditions. WINTER STAR MEDALLION has more cotton in it than any of my other quilts. It is a mix of 100% cottons and blends (cotton-polyester) because I could not get the colors desired in one type of blend. It is totally hand sewn – not because I think patchwork quilts should be hand sewn but because I enjoy hand sewing and feel I get my best results by this method."

"This quilt was my first experience with echo stippling. Having tried the straight line method (lines ⅛" apart) and not liking the effect, I used the echo idea. My echo quilting involves quilting along the design in rows ¹⁄₁₆" apart, much like Hawaiian quilting only closer. I like this method very much and have used it in my quilts since. Because it has a center of many pieces, I used a firmly woven cotton-polyester sheet for the back, to help keep the back from stretching and thus creating a pond or depression in the middle of my quilt."

The design for WINTER STAR MEDALLION, Annabel Baugher explains, "is an adap-

tation of Jinny Beyer's famous 'Ray of Light' medallion quilt." She adds, "Though there are some differences, they look very much alike in pictures. I named mine this because the colors and design remind me of winter in Missouri, where I have lived all my life."

Annabel explains, "My imagination does not go in patchwork design as it does in whole-cloth design. Thus, I am dependent upon other people's ideas and develop mine from this base. I am always careful to give the designer credit for the basic design as will, I hope, those who base their ideas on mine. God gave us all talents and created us individuals that we might compliment one another. I feel this is a way of sharing with each other. I have been very pleased with the results and take this opportunity to thank Jinny Beyer for a lovely design."

Speaking of her experiences with the quilt, Annabel says, "When it was entered in the AQS show there were those who were offended because it was a 'borrowed' idea. This has saddened me....I in no way wish to take away from the original designer rightful credit for the design. I only wish to compliment; I

*"I appreciate the support my family and friends give me –
especially my husband, Dale, who patiently waits for late, hurriedly
prepared meals, and carefully steps over miles of paper and cloth
and overlooks the dust on the furniture."*

WINTER STAR
MEDALLION
86" x 96"
1984
Annabel Baugher

WINTER STAR MEDALLION also tied for the 1985 Viewer's Choice Award.

liked the design enough to use it as a base for a quilt I wished to make. Because of this response, WINTER STAR MEDALLION is not entered in competitive shows now."

Annabel's advice to other quiltmakers: "When you enter your work in competition, follow all rules of the competition carefully and be willing to accept the judges' decision graciously, even though you personally may not agree."

Velda E. Newman
Nevada City, California

Iris

Velda E. Newman says she "loves working in flower gardens, and grows irises, among other flowers." The irises in her gardens inspired this 1985 award-winning quilt.

She adds, "I want to achieve a realistic look in my quilts." When she couldn't find the fabric she wanted to represent the flowers in this quilt, she used controlled

first place

1985 AQS Show & Contest
Applique, Amateur

bleaching and dyeing to create the exact fabrics she needed. There are no prints in this quilt; those that look like prints are actually fabrics which have been bleached or dyed.

The quilt is entirely appliqued, and with her applique, Velda also strives for realism, using fine detail work in areas such as the sword ferns.

Velda was an art major in college and has sewn since a child. Speaking of her background, she says, "I started quilting by making tradi-

tional pieced designs. I was not good at matching points. Then I found that I didn't have to do these traditional patterns — and if appliqueing, I didn't have to match the points. When I discovered that, I began to put all of my energy into quilting. When making original design applique quilts, I could do both my loves — sewing and art — at the same time." Velda lives in a small town, and says "Entering competitions and attending shows is a way of being involved with other quilters."

She says her main concern is color: "I am always

looking for new color combinations, in a realistic sense. I constantly explore color in my quilts, and I hope that each of my quilts is better than the last."

In her advice to other quiltmakers she again emphasizes the importance of color. "I really feel that the color is most important element. That is what draws someone to a quilt first — not the fine stitches or pattern. A lot of people hurry color development up. They settle for less than they want. I recommend that quiltmakers keep trying to find the exact color, or improvise and make it."

Velda always intends to make a smaller quilt, but "the designs invariably evolve into large and more involved quilts which take over a year to do." As a result, she is usually only able to enter the AQS show every other year.

IRIS
84" x 102"
1985
Velda E.
Newman

Arlene Statz
Sun Prairie, Wisconsin

Clamshell

To create the design of this award-winning quilt, Arlene Statz "used a small clamshell pattern for the quilt and a half circle pattern for the border." The entire quilt is made of 100% cotton, preshrunk fabric. About the construction, Arlene says, "I hand appliqued the small clamshells to long strips of fabric. All is hand quilted, using the clamshell for the

second place

1985 AQS Show & Contest
Applique, Amateur

quilting design on the solid background."

Arlene describes herself as a "farmwife" and "mother of five grown children." Talking about her activities, she says, "I do some gardening, but quilting is my favorite hobby. I am a member of AQS and the Prairie Heritage Quilters. I attend quilt classes during the fall and winter months, and I volunteer for charity projects in the community."

Speaking of CLAMSHELL, Arlene comments, "If you like hand work, this quilt is not that difficult. In using

the strip method it is very easy to adapt your quilt to different bed sizes."

Arlene says she doesn't feel any differently about CLAMSHELL now than she did when she made it. She continues, "I made it specifically for my bedroom but am delighted to have it hanging in the AQS museum so other people can enjoy it."

Talking about the award, she says, "Winning in the AQS show put me in the professional category. Now I feel I need to work harder if I am to compete in this category, even though there are some very talented quilters in the amateur category. On the local scene I am called 'the quilt lady' since I have won many awards on a number of my quilts."

To other quiltmakers Arlene says, "Go for it; not all can be winners,
but it is satisfying to just have a quilt hung with the best in the country."

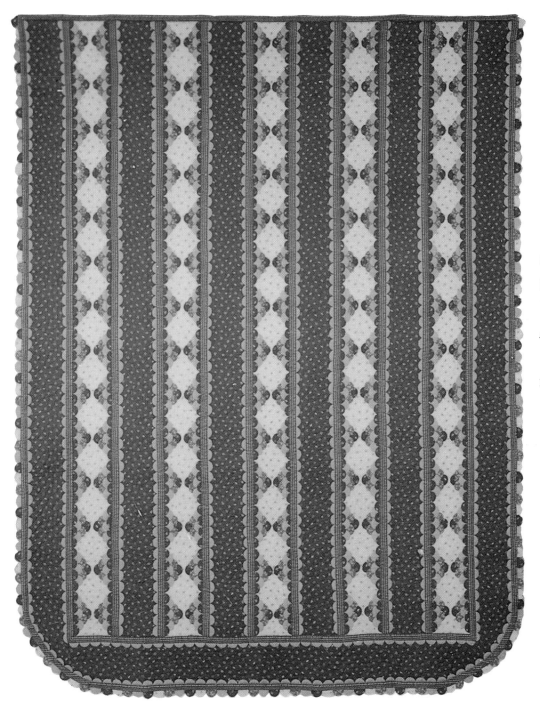

CLAMSHELL
84" x 104"
1984
Arlene Statz

Museum of AQS Collection

Carol Parker Hornback
Edwardsville, Illinois

Mallards

Carol Parker Hornback says this quilt "was a college graduation gift for my daughter who is an avid bird watcher and who taught me to be one also. On the back of the quilt I cross-stitched a verse to her. The sentiment in the verse, which was inspired by some of my thoughts and feelings about watching her grow up, is as important to me as the visual design of the quilt.

third place

1985 AQS Show & Contest Applique, Amateur

Carol has spent most of her adult life in Illinois. She has taught and is now a school counselor in Granite City, IL. Her interests center around "education, and a variety of areas related to artistic expression - particularly visual arts, literature, and philosophy, as well as areas related to the women's movement and women's rights."

About her AQS experience she says, "Making the quilt and entering it in the AQS competition led to some unexpected and pleasant surprises:

winning awards and recognition, and having pictures of it published. Best of all, it led to making many new friends, and to discovering an art form that has provided me with a satisfying form of self-expression. I believe that most of us, quiltmakers or not, are artists of sorts who find ways to show each other how we see the world. By participating in the AQS competition and in other exhibits, I have had the opportunity to enjoy and be inspired by the creative and supportive spirit I find in other quiltmakers."

She continues, "I have also become more appreciative of quilting as an art form and

have become more interested in the history of quilting. While there are many traditional patterns and motifs used in quilting, rarely are there two quilts alike. I think that many quilts are truly works of art, just as paintings and sculpture are."

"This experience," she adds, "has also heightened my interest in the role that quilts have played in the lives of women. It is almost as if quilting could be thought of as a metaphor for the way women (and men for that matter) have learned to take situations in their lives over which they seemed to have little control or situations that seemed to be lacking in possibilities, and use their creative energies toward positive and productive outcomes."

"On a more emotional level, quilting and quilts hold many charms for me and evoke warm memories and feelings. One of my repeated impressions of handmade quilts is that they are expressions of love and caring – with every single stitch put in place by a living, breathing person, usually for someone important and close to that person."

"Life is too short to make all the quilts a devoted quilter would like to make, so make the special ones, the ones you are willing to put your whole heart into."

MALLARDS
77" x 100"
1983
Carol Parker
Hornback

To Karen Hornback,
On Your Graduation

When you were a baby
I cradled your head
And rocked you gently
And tucked you in bed.

With the dreams of a mother
I watched to see
How you would grow
And who you would be.

Now you're a woman
Beautiful and grown
My dreams have come true
And you have dreams of your own.

I stitched you a quilt
Under which to lie
To nourish those dreams
As the nights idle by.

If ever you're tired or lonely or blue
Cuddle up in its folds for an hour
Or two
And once again
Let me comfort you.

B. J. Elvgren
Chesapeake, Virginia

The Twelve Days Of Christmas

B. J. Elvgren explains that THE TWELVE DAYS OF CHRISTMAS "attempts to catch the spirit of Christmas and comment that the gift of the Christ-child be central to that spirit."

She continues, "The inspiration for THE TWELVE DAYS OF CHRISTMAS was the traditional song, along with the self-appointed challenge of using a design to contain the

first place

1985 AQS Show & Contest
Applique, Professional

twelve groups within one scene. The Madonna and Christ-child were added as a comment on the foundation of gift-giving at Christmas." B. J. adds that after "carting the completed design and fabric around England for three months," she "finally began to get 'cooking' in her home studio in Pittsburgh."

The quilt took B. J. four months to complete and received the People's Choice Award at Quilt National '83.

About awards, she says, "Receiving recognition is always a great encouragement and stimulus to continue with new quilts. I was also very pleased to find it had inspired other quilters to try new projects." She adds, looking back at her quilt, "I still feel proud of it!"

B. J. is a folk artist working in the textile medium. Her love of fabric and sewing skills led her to begin quilting in 1979. B. J.'s works are exhibited throughout the nation and hang in many private collections. One of her largest commissioned pieces is WQED's 30TH ANNIVERSARY (22' x 10'), which celebrates that Pittsburgh station's contributions to the community.

Speaking to other quilters, she says: "You need to work to please yourself first. If you are satisfied with the quilt, that's more important than winning a competition. But, also, think about how a piece could have been improved. Go to shows, see what other quilters are doing and look critically to learn ways to improve your own work."

"My ambition continues to be to create art that is enriched by a strong folk heritage and that is a celebration of the wholeness of God's creation."

THE TWELVE
DAYS OF
CHRISTMAS
102" x 108"
1983
B. J. Elvgren

Museum of AQS Collection

Judy Simmons
Marietta, Georgia

Paradisier

Judy Simmons says of her background, "I've been sewing since I was five – doll clothes. I loved my mother's scrap box. I always loved paper dolls, fabric and new boxes of crayons. To this day, I still get a thrill opening a new box of crayons, and I find myself sneaking over to the children's book section, browsing through paper dolls (pretending to be buying them for my children). I've always loved color and fiber and was des-

second place

1985 AQS Show & Contest
Applique, Professional

tined to pursue this wonderful art form both in quiltmaking and wearable art. I am a home economist and taught sewing for years. I come from a long line of sewers including a great grandmother who made costumes for theater. I've always been exposed to fabric and sewing. It's in my blood! I thank God it is!"

The design for PARADISIER is Judy's own. Judy comments, "It's a very realistic, free-flowing design of the Birds of Paradise and all the magnificent plumage known to them. It's very heavily hand quilted, and lots of intricate applique

(such as the vines) ties it together and gives it a delicate look." Judy adds, "I love birds and flowers, which also provide endless subject matter. I love subtleness in color and design and feel most comfortable with it. I'm a lover of detail in all art forms, and I put a lot of detail in my quilts and wearables."

Discussing the development of PARADISIER, Judy says, "At one point I was totally upset with the look of the quilt. After all the applique had been done, I decided it needed a more subtle look, so I made a tea bath in my washing machine and submerged the whole quilt in it. It was 'do or dye/die!' I knew I would be throwing the quilt out or totally pleased.

Fortunately, it was the latter. I'm very intense about my work and I'm never afraid to take chances on anything — even risk complete failure.

"After making PARADISIER, I was very pleased with it. As time goes on I become more critical of it and see things in it I wish I had done differently. However, I am more sentimentally attached to this piece than any other I have done. It has received a lot of attention and I've met many nice people as a result. Perhaps that's why I'm sentimental about it. I've had offers to buy the quilt but cannot part with it.

Judy's advice to quiltmakers: "I have always told all my students from beginners on up to dive right in and enter all competitions. You'll never

*"I know I'll never achieve my masterpiece,
but hopefully I will come closer with each piece I create."*

PARADISIER
48" x 72"
1985
Judy Simmons

know unless you try. Judges' critiques are very beneficial and should be taken as such. I also feel it's so important for new quilters to share their work. Many beginning quilters have an easier time relating to a new quilter's work. I have always felt I never wanted to look back on something with regret at not doing it. I've got to feel at least I tried."

Glenys Nappo
Oak Ridge, Tennessee

Victorian Tulips

Glenys Nappo developed the design for this stained glass applique quilt "using patterns & designs in a Dover publication of stained glass designs." She adds, "I created this quilt because of my love for quilting and my love for stained glass windows."

third place

1985 AQS Show & Contest
Applique, Professional

This quiltmaker was so motivated to bring together these two loves that she taught herself to applique in order to recreate the window in fabric. The resulting quilt is of 100% cottons and is totally hand-appliqued and hand-quilted.

Speaking of her background, Glenys says, "I took a quilting class in 1980, which was a birthday present to myself, and I was immediately hooked. VICTORIAN TULIPS was my first and only full-size quilt finished." She continues, "I have been a member of Smoky Mountain Quilters for 10 years. I have not been able to do much for past four years because of arthritis in my hands, but I still love to look at beautiful quilts."

When I was finishing VICTORIAN TULIPS, I was under a lot of pressure to finish it for the 1983 National Quilting Association show in Bell Buckle, TN, and was tired of looking at it. When I look at it now, I'm amazed that I actually made it. I love VICTORIAN TULIPS, and am very proud of it."

Asked about the effects of her AQS award for VICTORIAN TULIPS, Glenys comments, "The awards I have won with this quilt have given me a greater sense of self-worth and confidence in my abilities."

"Don't be afraid to enter competitions. The criticisms can be very constructive. A great deal of satisfaction can be gained by sharing something you have created."

VICTORIAN
TULIPS
84" x 94"
1983
Glenys Nappo

Caryl Bryer Fallert
Oswego, Illinois

Through The Gazebo Window

This quilt is Caryl's interpretation of some favorite images in her surroundings, "including lattice, Victorian architectural details, a garden with spring flowers and fruit trees in bloom, and the unobstructed horizons of the rural Midwest." She tried to create "a fabric landscape with a very literal three-dimensional foreground, fading into a more abstract background."

first place

*1985 AQS Show & Contest
Other Techniques, Ama*

To make the quilt, she drew it full size, traced individual blocks, and then constructed it block by block. The piecing took three months and the hand quilting an additional two months.

For as long as she can remember, Caryl has expressed herself through artwork. She studied design, color and studio painting at Wheaton College (B.A.) and at several other universities.

About winning this award, Caryl comments, "At the time I made this quilt, I was relatively new to quiltmaking.

The AQS award and publication led to other invitations to exhibit my quilts, and to invitations from a number of quilt groups to lecture and teach. It was the quilt that made it possible for me to move from amateur to professional." Caryl currently exhibits her works in juried shows and lectures and conducts workshops worldwide. In 1986 this quilt was awarded the National Quilting Association's Masterpiece Quilt Award.

She says of competitions, "I believe that quilt competitions play an important role in raising the public consciousness about quilts. They

also provide an opportunity for quiltmakers to exhibit their work. They challenge us to do the best work we possibly can, both in design and in craftsmanship, and to complete our projects in a reasonable length of time."

She adds, "At the same time I do not think that it is a good thing for a quiltmaker to make a quilt solely for the purpose of entering a contest. I believe that quiltmakers should always make the quilts that come from the heart, the ones they most want to make. I don't think that any quiltmaker ought to compromise designs or ideas just to fit the rules of a particular contest."

"After many years of painting, sewing and dabbling in other media, I discovered that fabric, as an artistic medium, best expressed my personal vision."

THROUGH
THE GAZEBO
WINDOW
62" x 86"
1985
Caryl Bryer
Fallert

June Culvey
Garden Prairie, Illinois

Tranquil Violets

Asked about her background, June Culvey says she "learned quilting from grandmother" but is "self taught in other areas of quilting." She says she has often "drawn inspiration from Hallmark artists" and adds, "Two of my quilts are included in archives of Hallmark Cards in Kansas City, MO." Her quilts have also been featured in many maga-

second place

*1985 AQS Show & Contest
Other Techniques, Ama*

zines and won first place awards in a number of national shows. She says, though, "I do not sell, teach or lecture on quilts. I am a quilter and am very comfortable with this."

June says of her quilt, "TRANQUIL VIOLETS was made for my husband Daniel because I love him. I chose violets because, as the saying goes – 'Violets are forever.' That's how we feel about our marriage. I wanted a smooth uncluttered top

with a lot of quilting to gracefully enhance it. I tried to make it a quiet, elegant quilt. I liked it when I finished it and feel the same about it today. The colors are not loud or offensive so we can 'live' with this quilt for some time."

June says the design was adapted from a star pattern in *Quilter's Newsletter Magazine*, and the violet baskets were of her own designs. The quilting is freehand, and the colors were chosen from a Hallmark greeting card. Embroidery was done with a

single strand of embroidery thread, and she included tatting made by Lucinda Wheeler. About the quilting, June says, "I never mark a quilt for quilting before it goes into frame. I roll to the center and start. I never know how it will look until it comes off the frame. The large feathers I drew freehand as I came to that area."

Winning an award has affected June's work. She comments, "It has made me strive to produce the best quality quilt I can. When you win in any contest, it seems to make people take a closer look at what you can do."

In response to a request for advice for other quilt-makers, June explains, "I make quilts for my family and chosen friends. I spend a year or two with each project. I want these people to know that I believe they are worth this amount of time and effort. Even if you don't win any ribbons on your quilts, to have them shown in such a dignified quality show as the AQS presents is a compliment to your soul."

"Being a housewife doesn't get rave reviews (even as important as I consider it to be) but produce an award-winning quilt and people seem to sit up and take notice."

TRANQUIL
VIOLETS
92" x 96"
1984
June Culvey

Rumi O'Brien
Middleton, Wisconsin

The Journey Home

Rumi says about THE JOURNEY HOME, "I created this quilt out of frustration when I hurt my feet and was limited in activities. The fellow in the quilt is actually, literally, my spirit running for me."

The figures in the quilt are appliqued on a pieced background. The quilt is constructed entirely of cotton, and a double strand of

third place

*1985 AQS Show & Contest
Other Techniques, Ama*

embroidery floss was used as quilting thread.

Recently Rumi received a letter from a friend whom she and her husband had visited. This friend had enclosed several pictures which she had taken during that visit. Rumi says she discovered, "One (*shown right*) was a picture of me looking at a funny letter I had sent to my friend's children to explain with illustrations about THE JOURNEY

HOME – that was a long time ago and I had forgotten that I had written such a letter!"

Born in Tokyo, Japan, Rumi came to America when she was in her late teens, and later attended John Herron Art School in Indianapolis.

Speaking of quiltmaking, Rumi says, "Quilting is only a part of lots of things I do and I am not a productive quilter. I display no quilts in the house. I like to live in a very empty

house – seasonal changes that can be seen through the windows are the ornaments."

Asked to give advice to other quiltmakers, Rumi says, "Neatness is the most important thing in quiltmaking. It shows proper respect for the materials one uses. In my opinion the size of stitches doesn't matter as so often emphasized in quilt books. The size of stitches can be quite a tool for expression."

Rumi took the shape of the boy from Origami, the Japanese art of paper folding. As a child living in Japan, Rumi made the boy-shape, and has always been fascinated by the simple form.

THE JOURNEY
HOME
80" X 80"
1984
Rumi O'Brien

Annabel Baugher
Galt, Missouri

Peacocks

Annabel Baugher says "the idea for PEACOCKS came when I found a triangular quilting design with flying birds, grapes and vines in the book *The Romance of the Patchwork Quilt in America* by Carrie A. Hall and Rose G. Kretsinger." PEACOCKS is her own design, which developed from "many months of gathering bits and pieces from hither and yon" which "came together" in her mind. She adds that "three

first place

1985 AQS Show & Contest Other Techniques, Pro

more months were required to get it from head to hands to paper into a workable pattern."

This was Annabel's first attempt to design a quilt "mostly from non-quilting patterns." Annabel comments, "With nine large peacocks, small flying birds, clusters of grapes and vines, it seemed to be a very busy piece. When it was on paper only and even after it was drawn on the cloth (100% polyester Coupe-De-Ville), I was reasonably content, except for the fear of busyness. But when it was in the quilting frame, stretched and ready for those first

stitches, I knew a time of very real fear, bordering on terror. It suddenly dawned on me that once those stitches were placed in it, there was no turning back. But as the work progressed it was very satisfying to see the quilt develop much as I had visualized in my mind."

"This quilt has been entered in 17 competitive shows all over the USA and has placed first in its class in all except two and it placed in these also. It was supposedly finished in 1981. At that time it did not have the stipple quilting on it. I was not at all satisfied with the result. The areas around the small flying birds, grapes, and vines that were too small for the chosen background quilting of the rest

of the quilt. I was very disappointed. In 1984 I put it back into the quilting frame and did the stipple quilting and improved it 100%. This brought not only this part of the design out into a bold relief but the entire design seemed to stand out much better."

About the award, Annabel says, "Making this quilt has helped me gain confidence to act upon my own ideas. It has also made me more aware that in a whole-cloth quilt, design and workmanship are my only support. There is nothing else such as color, figure in fabric, or geometric shape for support. The quilts including this one have opened many doors for me and not only me but my husband as well. We have met so many wonderful people and

*"My quilts are all works of love for my family.
My goal is to leave a legacy of quilts of good design and excellent
workmanship to my family and whoever may see them in the future."*

PEACOCKS
88" x 96"
©1984
Annabel Baugher

gone many places we would not have gone otherwise. Of the many shows PEACOCKS has been in, the 1985 AQS and the 1988 show at Woodlawn plantation, where it received Best Quilting award, were the most exciting. AQS because it was the first one after the stipple work was done. Woodlawn because it was displayed on Nellie Custis Lewis' (Martha Washington's granddaughter's) huge four-poster bed!"

Annabel's advice to quiltmakers: "Do not be a slave to so called 'basic standards of quiltmaking.' Use or incorporate your own ideas into every quilt you make. Do the best you can every day and, knowing it is your best, be happy with it, though this need not be your best tomorrow."

Janice R. Streeter
Virginia Beach, Virginia

3-D Pine Tree

Janice R. Streeter was born in Sioux City, Iowa, but grew up in the Pacific Northwest and moved to Virginia in 1965. About her involvement in quilting she explains, "I began quilting in 1977. Traditional quilts helped me refine and improve my skills. I was never taught to quilt, so I did what seemed natural to me. This resulted in the develop-

second place

1985 AQS Show & Contest Other Techniques, Pro

ment of a unique style."

Speaking of 3-D PINE TREE she says the "original, three-dimensional design consisting of trees constructed using strips and prairie points came about as a result of my interest in self-expression, prairie points, and surface texture. The background and backing are unbleached muslin; the trees and border are green print. The blocks are 12" square; strips and prairie points are used to form the actual tree, which has an appliqued trunk and a row of prairie

points at the bottom to simulate a flower bed. The quilting design was inspired and adapted from a *Quilter's Newsletter Magazine* design."

Looking back at the quilt, Janice says, "I was so involved with working out the actual pattern that I don't think I spent enough time on the color scheme, which I now think could have been more interesting."

About the effects of entering competitions Janice comments, "I have learned a lot about myself and my personality. Entering competitions has given me self-confidence and pride in my work. To me, it is an important

means of self-expression of my individuality and interests. I have learned that I am a perfectionist very concerned with details, like to do things my own way (whether it is the accepted way or not), and have patience and perserverance (qualities needed to finish a quilt). It is gratifying when others enjoy the results of my efforts as much as I do."

To others Janice advises: "If you have an idea, don't be afraid to experiment with it. Precision is important. Don't settle for less than the very best that you can do. Each competition provides an opportunity to learn."

"This quilt was my first attempt at an original design. I thought that it was a neat idea and was very surprised at other people's favorable reaction to it."

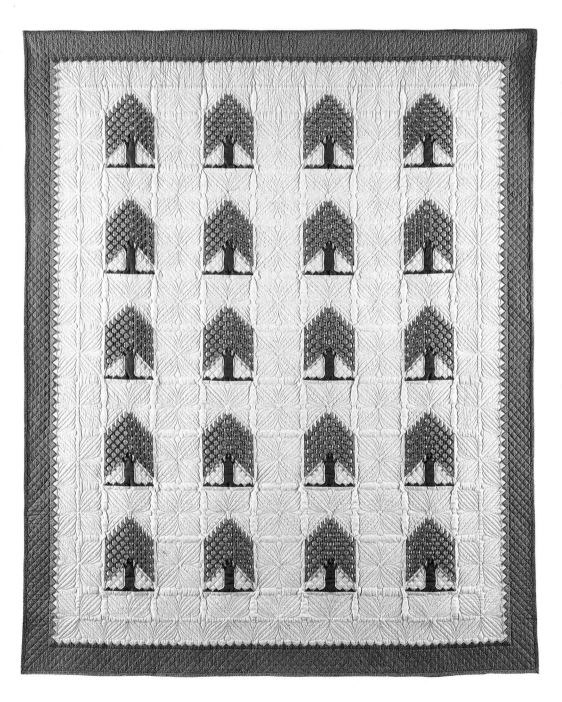

3-D PINE TREE
86" x 103"
1982
©1982
Janice R.
Streeter

Julia Needham
Knoxville, Tennessee

Wintergreen

About quilting, Julia Needham says, "Quilting is strictly a pleasurable hobby which has rewarded me with many unexpected honors, my two proudest being the AQS Gingher Award in 1988 and being awarded NQA Masterpiece status for WINTERGREEN in 1986. My inspiration, encouragement, and motivation all come from my dear friends, the Smoky Mountain Quilters."

third place

1985 AQS Show & Contest Other Techniques, Pro

She adds, "This quilt and all I've ever made are entirely my own. I have no input from any one." Its basic block, Mountain Pink, is an "obscure design" Julia found in *The Romance of the Patchwork Quilt in America* by Carrie A. Hall and Rose Kretsinger.

Never having seen the block used in a quilt in any show, book, or magazine, she says the block "piqued my curiosity and challenged my imagination."

Julia hand pieced her quilt using 100% cottons in various shades of greens, and used a striped border fabric in the sashing and the Streak of Lightning border. The intersections of the sashing are accented with appliqued

stars which add to the delicate look of the basic block. Julia says, "The challenge of using a picture of one block to construct a whole quilt without any preconceived idea of what it should look like was quite a struggle. I hope to find someone else's interpretation some day."

Julia comments, "Winning with this quilt at AQS and other shows has boosted my self-confidence and self worth. I need to enter my quilts in shows for the judges' expert opinions. This is a learning tool for me." She adds, "It is impossible for me to evaluate my work. Self-doubt invariably creeps in. Workmanship, design, color, proportions, contrasts could be better. It is such a relief for the quilt to be judged; then I'll know if it has any merit. Response to WINTERGREEN has certainly been a welcomed surprise."

"Make the quilts that please you. Everyone has different abilities and preferences so exploit them and be happy that they are unique. One of the best compliments I receive – 'I always recognize your quilts.'"

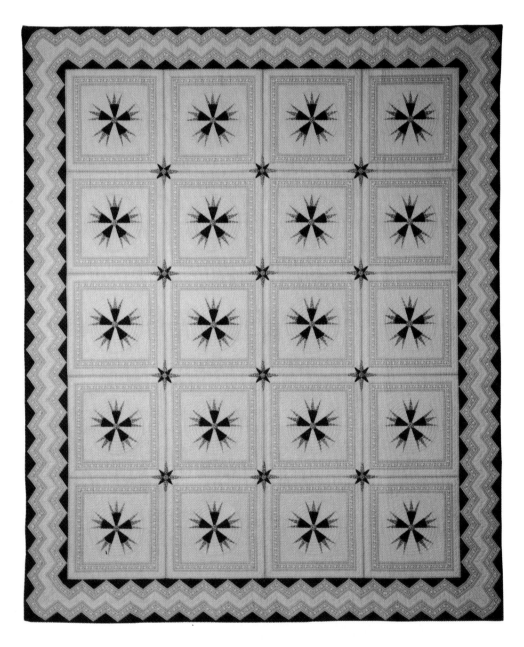

WINTERGREEN
77" x 92"
1984
Julia Needham

Miriam Nathan-Roberts
Berkeley, California

Lattice Interweave

About her quiltmaking, Miriam Nathan-Roberts says, "I am interested in creating illusions of three dimensions on the flat – or semi-flat surface. I had no depth perception until I was thirty years old."

She continues, "I tend to work on two series at once. The interweave series is very controlled and intellectual, I think. The structure is tight. I

first place

*1985 AQS Show & Contest
Group Quilt*

find that as I work on the interweaves, I need to rebel – to let loose. Thus was born the other series – I call it the architectural series – using wild fabrics, which I love, and very little pre-planning. The interweaves are very pre-planned. I tend to use a cool

palette and the same sense of space in both styles. Someday I hope to find a way to integrate the two series. People tend to associate my work with the interweaves (I always think this series is over, but then another one calls to me and it resurfaces) and don't think of the other series as my work."

Asked about the development of LATTICE INTERWEAVE, Miriam says, "My aim in this quilt was to achieve a sense of three dimensionality on a flat surface. I also wanted a contrast between the strong design element, devoid of color, against a background of color to make the grid appear to float in

front. It looks like bands of woven steel, to me."

This original-design quilt is constructed of cottons and blends, and is machine-pieced. It was hand quilted by Sarah Hershberger of Charm, Ohio.

Miriam holds a B.S. in home economics from Cornell University, with a concentration in clothing and design, and an M.A. in educational psychology from University of California, Berkeley. Her quilts have been included in many exhibitions and she has been winning awards for her work since 1980. Asked how she feels about the quilt now, Miriam comments, "I always like the quilt I finished most recently best."

Speaking of her AQS award, she explains, "It has helped me to take my quiltmaking seriously – it really helps my family to take my quiltmaking seriously."

"I am interested in structure and repeated images. Things lined up on shelves, stacks of logs, rows of equipment, etc. have always drawn me."

LATTICE
INTERWEAVE
80" x 80"
©1983
Miriam
Nathan-Roberts

Quilted by
Sarah
Hershberger

Rebekka Seigel, Owenton, Kentucky
Quilted by Carmen Prewitt, Corinth, Kentucky

The Twelve Dancing Princesses

Rebekka Seigel tells us THE TWELVE DANCING PRINCESSES is "based on the Grimm Brothers' fairy tale by the same name." She adds, "The imagery in this piece was inspired by a children's book that my grandmother read to me many times during my childhood." All designs used in the quilt are original designs by Rebekka.

Rebekka continues, "Techniques used in this piece

second place

1985 AQS Show & Contest Group Quilt

include applique, reverse applique, batik, seminole patchwork, direct dye, beading and embroidery. The quilt is constructed of cottons and blends with accents of gold lame for that fairy tale feeling. The quilt is entirely hand quilted by Carmen using buttonhole twist thread."

Of her background, Rebekka says, "I started making quilts in 1973 because I was expecting my first child and thought that was what mothers were supposed to do based on the example set for me in my life by my grand-

mother. Over the past 17 years I have experimented with many techniques and have discovered the outlet for creative expression in the art of quiltmaking." Rebekka has won many honors for her work in state and national competitions, and she is currently showing her work in gallery settings and teaching the art of quiltmaking to adults and children alike.

This is the largest piece Rebekka has ever made and it took her nine months to complete the top. Because Rebekka wanted to enter it in the AQS Show, Carmen quilted the entire 120" x 130" top in a month and a half, on a hoop, in her trailer. Asked about herself, Carmen Prewitt says,

"I am a self-taught quilter and have made several traditional quilts and quilted a lot for others, and feel honored to have done several for Rebekka. It is hard to get the quilts made for my family that I would like."

About the quilt Rebekka comments,"There are so many elements of the story worked into this piece that some are too small to be appreciate in an overall camera shot. Because this piece doesn't photograph well, I do not consider it one of my best efforts though it is one that is often remembered."

About the AQS award, Rebekka says, "Since this award came to me rather early in my quilting career, it cer-

Rebekka Seigel (left) and Carmen Prewitt

Rebekka comments, "I always like my work better after it has been out in the world awhile than I do when it is freshly finished.
My personal involvement with all the trials of the construction and imagery are too fresh in the beginning for me to be able to really like it."

THE TWELVE
DANCING
PRINCESSES
130" x 120"
1984
Rebekka Seigel

Quilted by
Carmen Prewitt

tainly helped me to form an image of myself as an award-winning quiltmaker and has encouraged me to go on making quilts that tell the stories of my life."

To other quiltmakers, Rebekka says: "Remember when entering your work in competition that all judging is subjective. Whether you win or lose, it is the decision of one or two particular persons. The next person who judges your work may have an entirely different response to it. Do your best, take pride in what you do no matter the outcome of the judging and above all, KEEP IT UP!"

The Associate Loyalist Quilters
Bath, Ontario, Canada

The Bath Bicentennial Quilt

Jessie Demaine, the designer of THE BATH BICENTENNIAL QUILT, says about the development of this quilt: "In 1784, the village of Bath, Ontario, was founded by Americans who had left their New England homes after the American Revolution. In 1984, the village celebrated its Bicentennial and residents were asked to initiate their own individual commemora-

third place

1985 AQS Show & Contest Group Quilt

tive projects. I personally was inspired by the lovely old houses of the village, a unique cluster of examples of early Canadian domestic architecture. Searching for a way to incorporate the street-scape into a cooperative project led to the idea of a quilt. Surely only a completely inexperienced quilter would dream of asking each of her equally inexperienced neighbors to do a block of the family home in appliqued detail, all to be combined in a quilt to grace the celebration! However, a few were interested."

She continues, "Then, by one of those incredible coincidences that shape events, I met Doris Waddell, a local quilter of great skill and dedication, a winner of many prizes in major competitions. She liked the idea of the quilt; she rallied support of experienced quilters in the area and the project was launched. The quilt was completed in time to be presented to the Village of Bath at the time of the Bicentennial celebrations. The quilt was eventually placed in the quilt collection of the Agnes Etherington Art Center, Queen's University, Kingston. When I see it on display now, I am really at a loss to focus my thoughts, or define my reactions. The quilt has won so many awards, and delighted so many viewers, it will commemorate this village and its

people in a very unique way for many years to come. If I were to design another theme quilt, there are some things I would do differently, such as integrating the lines of quilting in the individual blocks into a more cohesive pattern. But on balance, I am very happy to have shared in such a meaningful project."

Asked about the quilt, Doris Waddell says, "It continues to delight viewers, even six years after completion. As part of the Heritage Quilt Collection at the Agnes Etherington Art Centre, it surfaces from time to time in one of the centre's galleries (sometimes hanging alongside paintings) and also is available for loan to other galleries across Canada." She adds that it has won first prize at many regional and national shows.

"Doris Waddell, Associate Loyalist quilter: "When I see the quilt now, I still feel extremely proud of it and of the people involved in making it. As I drive around the village of Bath from time to time, the buildings depicted in the quilt have a special attraction for me."

THE BATH
BICENTENNIAL
QUILT
74" x 90"
1984
The Associate
Loyalist Quilters

Nineteen of the 20
Associate Loyalist
Quilters (1984)
are pictured on page 52.

Doris adds, "I thought at the time of the Bath quilt, I had reached the top of my quilting form, but I have continued to expand my horizons and with my newest effort, a Baltimore-style quilt taking about 4,000 hours of work – I now say 'It is the most worthwhile piece of work I've done.' The Bath quilt allowed that growth."

Carol Goddu
Mississauga, Ontario, Canada

Hesperides

Cotton eyelet, synthetic suede, assorted silk and silky dressmaker fabrics and velour are all a part of this exciting quilt based on an illustration for "I Saw Three Ships," found in a c.1900 children's book of nursery rhymes. Hand and machine applique were used by Carol to create layers of dimensional applique, free-standing figures, boats, sails,

first place

1985 AQS Show & Contest Wall Quilt, Amateur

which were then attached to the background in successive three-dimensional layers. Machine quilting, embroidery, and embellishments such as ribbons, braids and buttons contributed additional details.

Carol says of this quilt, "It was made for a wall in my bedroom and I enjoy seeing it there now as much as I did in 1984."

Having studied art history at Smith College in Northampton MA (B.A.) and Trinity College, Hartford CT (M.A.), Carol began quilting

in 1972, working from traditional patchwork patterns. In 1981 she began working in pictorial applique, in 1983 she began exhibiting her work, and in 1985 she began lecturing and teaching. Her quilts have appeared in many shows and many publications, and in 1986 she was the first quilter selected from Canada to design a garment for the Fairfield Processing Fashion Show.

"The 1985 AQS show," Carol tells us, was the first time that she had "packed up a quilt in a box and sent it away to a non-local show." She says of the experience, "I was pleased just to have it

accepted for exhibit and had no expectations of winning anything. When I did win, I used my prize money to attend Continental Quilting Congress – another first for me. And the rest of my resume follows from those experiences."

To other quiltmakers Carol suggests, "Follow your instincts – make the quilts you want to make the way you want to make them, even if a few 'rules' of traditional quiltmaking get bent in the process. Attend every show you have the oppportunity to see – read the new books and magazines; be inspired by what others are doing."

"I like sending this quilt out to shows and sharing it, but I really love having it come home again."

HESPERIDES
31" x 49"
1984
Carol Goddu

Barbara Temple
Marietta, Georgia

Endangered

Speaking of ENDANGERED, Barbara Temple says, "This quilt was done for my husband. I wanted to catch the sadness of a fading heritage and to show how mankind is endangering not only the eagle, but man himself. I came up with the design idea when I saw some paintings by an Arizona artist that combined wildlife and Indians' faces. They were so beautiful

second place

1985 AQS Show & Contest Wall Quilt, Amateur

together I felt I had to try and capture the strong emotions the paintings evoked. I developed the pattern from one of my drawings and then enlarged it."

The quilt was constructed with 100% cotton in solid colors and with four to five different values. Barbara "hand appliqued the entire piece and then quilted an Indian pottery design. Embroidery thread was used to enhance the eyes on the eagle and the Indians."

About her background, Barbara says, "I began quilting in 1983 when my dear friend, Judy Simmons, convinced me to try it. We attended a Chris Wolf-Edmonds seminar and I couldn't believe what could be done with quilting. I had always thought it was just patchwork like my grandmother had done. I have no background in quilting, just determination."

Barbara feels differently about the quilt now than she did when she first made it. She explains, "It was only my second attempt at quilting. There are many things I have learned now that I could have used to enhance the quilt and to give it more depth. You are so excited when you complete a quilt, but after you are done and away from it, you begin to critique it."

She says about her AQS experience, "I entered the show knowing I was a fool for doing so. After all, I had no background in quilting. But, I was proud of myself and the year I had put into this quilt. I wanted to share it. To have won a prize for it was a dream come true. I have to say I was in shock for months."

Her recommendations to other quiltmakers: "I hope they continue quilting so that everyone can share in all the love that goes into every one of their stitches."

"Don't be afraid to enter quilts in the shows. Being able to share in the wonderful creations brings much warmth and joyfulness to all of us. Besides, where do you think most of us get our next idea or inspiration?"

ENDANGERED
48" x 72"
1984
Barbara Temple

Barbara Lydecker Crane
Lexington, Massachussetts

Outlooks

Barbara Crane says of her involvement in quiltmaking, "I've always been interested in art and in sewing! Art was my favorite subject in school and my major at Skidmore College. For 15 years, I worked full or part time (freelance) in graphic design. When I discovered the 'art quilt' medium in 1980, I found the perfect outlet for my creative energy. Since 1985, I have been a pro-

third place

*1985 AQS Show & Contest
Wall Quilt, Amateur*

fessional quilter — selling work, lecturing, teaching, writing. My work has been included in many major exhibits and has been published in several books, magazines and catalogs."

OUTLOOKS is an original-design quilt made of cottons, some of which have been hand dyed. Both hand and

machine construction were used, but the quilting and stippling were all done by hand. Miniature animals and other objects embellish the surface of the quilt.

Describing the process of quilting OUTLOOKS, Barbara says, "I felt akin to a medieval stonemason as I laboriously hand quilted and stippled the gray striped background fabric into a 'wall' of 'stones.' Certainly it was tedious work, but very satisfying and

almost magical: I felt I had transformed cotton into stone. Also, if you, the viewer, feel claustrophobic or imprisoned, use the key provided and let yourself out."

As she looks back at the quilt, Barbara comments, "I still find it interesting and inventive, but I think my recent quilts are more visually exciting. The idea for this work came after a long (for me) dry spell, and its creation really refueled my spirit. Then, to have it not only accepted but also given an award by AQS, and then to have it subsequently purchased by them, was tremendously affirming. Around that time, I was longing to give up my graphic design work and plunge into quiltmaking professionally. The AQS award seemed like a signpost reading 'YES! GO!' and I went. It still seems like an excellent decision, perhaps one of the most important in my life."

Barbara advises other quiltmakers: "Study all the art you can. Try to make your work communicate, not merely decorate."

OUTLOOKS
60" x 54"
©1984
Barbara Crane

Museum of AQS Collection

Lucretia Romey
Canton, New York

Cityscape

A sketch of the skyline of Toronto made by Lucretia as she looked from the 7th floor of the Westbury Hotel was the inspiration for this striking quilt. She comments, "I have always liked city architecture and the geometry and design of groups of buildings. Usually I carry a sketch book, but this time I used the hotel stationery for the drawing."

She hand sewed the quilt,

first place

1985 AQS Show & Contest Wall Quilt, Professional

as she always does, using her direct "flip and sew" technique. Cottons, cotton blends and metallic fabrics were all used in the construction. As Lucretia looks at the quilt now, she comments, "I am a better 'sewer' now," and adds,

"I hope I continue to improve."

A fine arts degree from Indiana University and graduate work in silversmithing and sculpture are a part of this quiltmaker's background. She now exhibits both her art quilts and watercolors internationally, participating in juried and invitational shows. She adds that some of her quilts find their way into

her paintings – as backgrounds for flower still lifes.

Speaking of her AQS award, Lucretia comments, "It is always pleasant to know others find one's work worthwhile – whether the piece wins an award or is purchased or someone casually says they 'like' it."

Her message to other quiltmakers: "I hope to encourage my students and others to use their imagination and invent their own works of art. It is important to look around and be inspired by one's surroundings – whether by the shape of a bird's wing, the color of a flower or the geometry of a building. I hope my students will not be afraid of making "mistakes" and will try new combinations of colors and shapes and ways of doing things."

"All of my wall quilts are the result of my drawings done in my yard or while traveling. This quilt is one of a series of cityscapes that are now in private and corporate collections."

CITYSCAPE
50" x 64"
1984
Lucretia Romey

Museum of AQS Collection

Rosie Wade
Franklin, Tennessee

For All His Glory

Describing the subject of her quilt, Rosie Wade says, "On a Sunday night on their way home from church an Amish couple have stopped for a rest and prayer; the children are fast asleep in the back of the buggy. The Amish man has leaned forward to lead the prayer. The horse, sensing the peace, has bowed his head. The central focus is the sun which has a quilted

second place

1985 AQS Show & Contest Wall Quilt, Professional

crucifix showing Christ as the Light and big tremendous rays emitting from the sun, as if to say, prayers go up on a sunbeam and answers and grace come back on another sunbeam. The cattails mean hope for life everlasting. The rings on the water near the horse are the expression of quietness when we pray and hear the presence of God in all of creation."

"FOR ALL HIS GLORY,"

Rosie explains, "is my attempt at explaining the Amish lifestyle. The Amish are warm people centered on not being worldly and their color comes from nature; their focus is on their families and God." She adds, "All cotton solids were used because the Amish do not use print in any of their work and they believe prints are too worldly."

Looking back, Rosie says she laughs at "all the mistakes" she made, but appreciates the design more and more. She explains, "I'm beginning to see it in a different light. I am amazed at the length of time it took me to make this, only four or five weeks. This quilt just popped out. I drew this directly onto fabric with no pattern – ruler and a pencil in hand."

She continues, "I feel amazed that the work of our hands is such an expression of the times we are in. That time in my life was a rough one and this quilt helped me bridge my way across so many paths. It gave me better

self-esteem and helped me know my talents weren't a maybe. At the time, I didn't know how many people I would meet from entering the AQS show."

About her background, Rosie comments, "In 1982 the quilting instructor wasn't working out so my sister encouraged me to teach the class. And here I am in 1991, still teaching. I have a custom quilt business and have done quilts for everyone from people in Amsterdam to the Governor of Tennessee."

To other quiltmakers, she says, "Don't be afraid of letting go and saying something really profound; that expression will be an indication to you as your own witness, of how great it is to be a quilter and to use a needle, to let that expression surface. This same advice I teach my class because Martha Mullinix, my first quilting teacher said to me 'Remember, this is where I'm teaching you but this is the point of departure.' Amen! Go for it!"

The best advice I can give is to leave the ways you've been taught and go out into a direction that is truly your own. Let who you are and where you are sink down onto the canvas, your quilt.

FOR ALL HIS
GLORY
108" x 74"
1985
Rosie Wade

Moneca Calvert
Rocklin, California

Tropical Reef Fish

Moneca Calvert, a native Californian, says, "There were were no quilts in my formative years. I didn't know quilts were still being made until I was 20 years of age. Largely self-taught, I have over 40 years sewing experience. In 1982 I 'discovered' the current quilting world! My first class from Katie Pasquini happened quite by chance and that led to the further

third place

*1985 AQS Show & Contest
Wall Quilt, Professional*

discovery of related events such as shows, guilds, conferences and quilt publications and the knowledge that I, too, could be a part of it! Original design was being accepted – thinking I had to re-create the wonderful traditional patterns was one of the hurdles I had not conquered before 1982. Since then, I have consciously worked towards this "career" through judged competitions. I reasoned it was the fastest way to gain recognition for my style and contribution to quilting."

She continues, "I have

thoroughly explored the traditional clamshell pattern and tried to give it an update through size, piecing and placement. My preference leans towards curves and I have incorporated them in all my work whether it be clamshell, hearts, pictorials or whatever. I have received awards on all the quilts entered in competition and they are all special. I started teaching on a national level in 1985, and I am always aware of my good fortune to be actively creating and sharing QUILTS!"

In TROPICAL REEF FISH, large clamshells placed in

contemporary tessellation with a "spacer" template between clamshells create dimensional quilting. Color-wheel solids and prints that read as solids create the triangular focal point on a white-to-gray-to-black background. Talking about the work, Moneca says, "The quilt was created for use as a visual teaching aid for my clamshell workshops. It was greatly admired by everyone, especially men. It gave my work an enormous boost. I consider it the first of my most successful quilts."

She adds, "I had no idea how popular that quilt would be and still is! It won an award

"Enter competition ONLY if you can accept rejection. Try not to set yourself up for a huge disappointment. Judges cannot please everyone just as your work will not please everyone, and that's OK."

TROPICAL REEF
FISH
42" x 50"
©1984
Moneca Calvert

every time it was in competition." Unfortunately, it was one of six of Moneca's clamshell quilts which were stolen in June, 1986. She comments, "It suspect it remains the most popular piece in my clamshell series. I am asked about it repeatedly. Not knowing its whereabouts does give me a great sense of loss."

Marcy Jefferson & Other Quiltmakers
Dearborn, Michigan

Memories Of Clara

Most of the quilters who were involved in creating MEMORIES OF CLARA belonged to a local quilt group formed after having taken a beginning quilt class several years earlier. The idea of this group project was introduced to the group by Marcy Jefferson, who was then special projects assistant at the Henry Ford Estate and also a member of the group. Marcy tells us "The quilters repre-

Viewer's Choice

1985 AQS Show & Contest

sented a variety of ages and outside interests, but met twice a month to enjoy a common interest. The group recently disbanded; MEMORIES OF CLARA was their most ambitious project."

Marcy explains more about the project: "The quilt was based on a quilt owned by Henry and Clara Ford and originally used on the master bedroom sunporch. (The finished quilt is displayed at the Henry Ford Estate, now a National Historic Landmark on the campus of the University of Michigan-Dearborn.) Instead of trying to reproduce the quilt exactly, we decided to pick up on the sense of it –

we used the idea of birds and branches with an open background. The quilt resembles the original and represents the Fords' interest in wildlife. No specific pattern was used. Design ideas were influenced by a black and white photograph showing a corner of the quilt and the birds and floral elements used for the chintz applique."

She continues, "Because this was a group project and we wanted several people working on the hand applique at the same time, the quilt was constructed in five sections that were sewn together when the applique was finished. Some of the motifs that overlapped the seams were appliqued when the top was together. Much of the curved feather plumes and cross-hatched background hand quilting was done at the Estate on Sunday afternoons for tours. With the exception of the chintz, all fabric and supplies were donated by manufacturers and a Dear-

born quilt store."

Speaking of the quilt, Marcy says, "We were all pleased to be involved in the restoration of the Henry Ford Estate and believed our quilting efforts were a significant contribution. But, the quilt was also a monumental undertaking that occupied us for two years. Because of the extensive time commitment involved, completing it was a tremendous relief."

About the award, Marcy comments, "MEMORIES OF CLARA was not originally intended to be a competition quilt, but when the AQS show was announced, it provided the needed motivation to finish. Without the show deadline to keep us on schedule, we might still be quilting. Just being accepted to the show was gratifying, but winning was especially satisfying; it provided important recognition for us — for a job well done. Since this quilt is on display, we do receive very fine compliments from guests who have seen the quilt on the tour."

To other quiltmakers, Marcy says: "Success requires more than fine quiltmaking skills. Bring to the venture patience, enthusiasm, and a sense of humor."

"Some visitors to the estate see a bedcovering, some see a beautiful quilt, some recall memories of quilting mothers or grandmothers, some reflect on the Fords. I see tangible evidence of the commitment and the friendship of eleven women gathered together because of a love of quiltmaking."

MEMORIES
OF CLARA
102" x 84"
1985
Donna Aldrich
Cheryl Boyd
Karen Bullock
Cherie Cornick
Marlene Czerwick
Donna Hamilton
Deborah B. Hohner
Marcy Jefferson
Linda Jolly
Nan Suydam
Lauri Taylor

Clara Bryant Ford c. 1925.
From the collections of
Henry Ford Museum
& Greenfield Museum.

67

Quilt Show & Contest

1986

The second American Quilter's Society Quilt Show & Contest
was held May 2-4, 1986, at the Executive Inn Riverfront
in Paducah, Kentucky.

Judges for quilt awards were Patricia Morris, Glassboro, NJ;
Jean Ray Laury, Fresno, CA; and Aloyse Yorko, Tequesta, FL.
Categories and category award sponsors were as follows:

Best of Show, American Quitler's Society
Judges' Merit Award, American Quilter's Society
First Quilt, American Quilter's Society
Gingher Award for Excellence of Workmanship, Clair Gingher
Traditional Patchwork, Amateur, Hobbs Bonded Fibers
Traditional Patchwork, Professional, Coats & Clark

Innovative Patchwork, Amateur, Fairfield Processing Corp.
Innovative Patchwork, Professional, Gutcheon Patchworks
Applique, Amateur, V.I.P
Applique, Professional, Mountain Mist
Other Techniques, Amateur, Extra Special Products, Inc.
Other Techniques, Professional, White Sewing Machine Co.
Team Quilt, Amateur or Professional (2 people), American Quilter's Society
Group Quilt, Amateur or Professional (3 or more people), Swiss-Metrosene, Inc.
Wall Quilt, Amateur, Yours Truly/Burdett Publications
Wall Quilt, Professional, Fiskars

In each category three awards were made: 1st place, $700; 2nd place, $500; 3rd place, $200. The Gingher Award for Excellence of Workmanship was a $2,500 award; the AQS Best of Show Award, $10,000; and the First Quilt Award, $200.

The exhibit included 370 quilts representing 48 states, and Canada, France and Japan. During the show, many of the 10,000 people who attended voted for their favorite quilt, and a Viewer's Choice award was later made.

Faye Anderson
Denver, Colorado

Spring Winds

"Before making SPRING WINDS, all of my quilt designs had been bold and geometric," says Faye Anderson, the creater of this outstanding quilt. She says that with this quilt she "wanted to try something more traditional and charming." She adds, "There was no difference in the design approach; all of the same principles applied; only the fabrics and

best of show

1986 AQS Show & Contest

motifs changed. Good design is independent of style."

Faye says the center medallion was "sketched from a friend's Oriental carpet and sewn in a block for an applique contest in Chicago." Faye later "developed it into the wheel form for SPRING WINDS." She says "The idea for the birds' nests came from a quilt I'd seen in a museum in South Carolina; I was able to integrate them into the garland border."

Describing the quilt, Faye continues, "The quilt is unusual because of the print background. There are actu-

ally two prints, a positive and negative gray and white pattern used in the center and the border. The quilt is hand appliqued and hand quilted. The brown points on the wheel and border are appliqued, not pieced, which for me is easier. The quilting is in swirls to represent the air currents that carry the birds."

Originally from the Chicago area, Faye has lived in Colorado for 27 years, since moving there to complete her BFA in graphic design at the University of Denver. She "discovered quilting in 1980 by taking a sampler class," and says she vacillates between designing

traditionally-styled and more contemporary quilts and wearables. She adds, "My other passion, besides quilting, is travel to study other cultures and the art and textiles they produce."

Talking with other quiltmakers about competitions, Faye says: "Personally, I have been rejected from as many shows and competitions as I have been accepted into. The rejections make me work harder to grow and expand my vision, even if I thought the rejected work was as good or even superior to some of the works accepted. Rejections are depressing and perplexing, but fortunately for quiltmakers, there

"Winning this award gave me a LOT of confidence in my sewing and design skills – and helped me think of myself as an 'artist' and of quilting as an art-form."

SPRING WINDS
76" x 87"
©1985
Faye Anderson

Museum of AQS Collection

is always another show to enter! Winning awards is not simply a matter of 'luck,' but does involve such a combination of factors (the taste of the jurors, the number of entries and categories, the type of show, etc.) that when the points are totalled it can seem more like luck than anything else!"

Karin Matthiesen
Madison, Wisconsin

Bed of Peonies

Speaking of her background, Karin Matthiesen says, "I grew up in Oconomowoc, Wisconsin, the eldest of seven children. I began quilting in 1971 at the age of 18. I was inspired by a quilt pattern I saw in *Good Housekeeping* magazine. It was an applique quilt, something I never would have attempted had I known what I was doing. I worked on this quilt off and on for seven

ginger award

for workmanship
1986 AQS Show & Contest

years. During that time I got married, moved to Madison and began taking quilt classes."

Karin continues, "I won several ribbons on that first quilt. I have gone on to make 11 other full-size quilts, 10 or 12 crib quilts, several wall-hangings and many pillows. Most of the items I make are for gifts, although I've sold a few things."

About this award-winning quilt, Karin says, "I made BED OF PEONIES for the 1986 Mountain Mist contest, using a Mountain Mist pattern. I began it in early September 1985 and finished it the day I had to mail it to the contest one year later. The flowers are pieced, and the leaves and stems are appliqued. The quilting pattern is also a Mountain Mist design, and the background quilting is ¼" apart." Karin adds, "The pattern was a challenge, with its large amount of quilting, many points and much applique."

Looking at the quilt now, she says, "It was worth every stitch I put into it." About the award Karin won, she comments, "It's given me more confidence as a quiltmaker, and an appreciation of how much influence luck has on our lives."

"I feel my strong point in quilting is workmanship. I'm more comfortable adapting existing patterns than I am creating original designs."

BED OF
PEONIES
85" x 96"
1986
Karin
Matthiesen

Museum of AQS Collection

Judy Anne Walter
Chicago, Illinois

No Unnecessary Floating

Speaking of NO UNNECESSARY FLOATING, Judy Anne Walter says, "This is quilt number 19 in a long series of quilts based on Islamic designs. When I made this quilt, I had just begun using a wall board for designing my quilts. I like the freedom this gives me: I cut and pin, take pieces out, put new pieces in. I like to use a wide variety and number of fab-

judges' merit
Award
1986 AQS Show & Contest

rics in my quilts – working on the wall helps me get the effects I want."

This quilt "inspired by a portion of an Islamic design" is constructed of "commerical, hand-dyed, and discharged (machine-bleached) cottons, velvets, velveteens, taffeta, satin, poly-cotton blends," and is "machine-pieced, hand-appliqued and hand-quilted."

Judy Anne Walter's quilts have been shown nationally in group, invitational and juried exhibits and are included in several corporate and private collections. She has designed wearable art for several Fairfield Fashion Shows, including the 1988 "Superstar Show." Her work has appeared in numerous

PHOTO: LARRY BOLE

books and magazines. Judy travels nationally to give workshops and lectures at quilt guilds and conferences and in Illinois as part of the Illinois Artist-in-Education Program. Judy is the author of *Creating Color: A Dyer's Handbook.*

About the effect of her AQS show experience, Judy says, "The month I won the award for NO UNNECESSARY FLOATING, I also was named 'Teacher of the Year' by *Professional Quilter* magazine. This double set of honors was a wonderful personal achievement for me as a quilt artist and instructor. Winning this pair of awards paved the way for me to offer workshops and lectures nationally."

"I encourage all quiltmakers to enter competitions in order to give others a chance to see their work and to get feedback on it from judges, the public, etc. Competitions give us personally an opportunity to grow and offer new inspirations and ideas to those who come to see the work."

NO
UNNECESSARY
FLOATING
73" x 73"
©1986
Judy Anne
Walter

Barbara Pettinga Moore
Shelburne, Vermont

Buffalo Magic

"The patterns used in BUFFALO MAGIC," explains Barbara Pettinga Moore, "are original adaptations of American Indian bison symbols. The artifacts upon which the symbols are found belong to numerous museum collections and include shields, drums, hide paintings, sun dance effigies, beadwork and one ancient Mimbres pottery figure. This first quilt was born of five consuming inter-

first quilt

Award
1986 AQS Show & Contest

ests: bison, natural history museums, sewing, travel and several summers spent in bison country as a park ranger in Badlands and Yellowstone National Parks."

Describing the development of the quilt, Barbara says, "BUFFALO MAGIC is hand-appliqued and hand-quilted. The suede cloth figures are sewn to cotton broadcloth. Geometric designs painted on Plains Indian parfleches, or carrying cases, suggested the patchwork of the inner border. All hand quilting represents designs and configurations accompanying each bison artifact or

was selected from other artifacts attributed to that particular tribe."

Speaking of her background, Barbara says, "My Maine childhood was rural. During twelve early years on a dairy farm I experienced my first interest in bovines, our herd of Guernsey cattle. Much later, following several years of rapid transitions as the wife of Bob Pettinga, a young military pilot, we settled in Northwestern Vermont 31 years ago and have stayed here. Our five children came first; later I earned an undergraduate degree in art education and a master of science degree in education with a botany specialty. My eclectic and late-blooming career includes teaching art, free-

lance writing, natural history lecturing, museum exhibit design and consulting. The past few years have marked another period of rapid changes; Bob's unexpected death in Yellowstone National Park in the much-publicized wildfire summer of 1988 ended nearly 35 years of marriage. The following summer, also in Yellowstone, I married Don Moore, a high school earth science teacher. 1990 has been a resettlement year. Now, finally established I am contemplating a new quilt; its theme – grizzly bears."

Asked what she would like people to know about this quilt, Barbara says, "This quilt introduced me to a new art form, quiltmaking, as a means of visual expression. BUFFALO MAGIC and all its spin-offs have been a highly-educational and rewarding experience – almost a journey." About her current feelings for the quilt, she says, "I am less critical of it than I was. Upon its completion I initially found it difficult to view it in its entirety because I was somewhat bogged down in its details and flaws."

Barbara comments on her award: "Although the AQS and other competitions took place several years ago I am still

*Barbara encourages quiltmakers: "Trust your creative instincts.
Do not be afraid to break new ground. Believe that whatever you don't
know how to do you can learn. Above all, pay attention to detail –
strive towards excellence in terms of craftsmanship."*

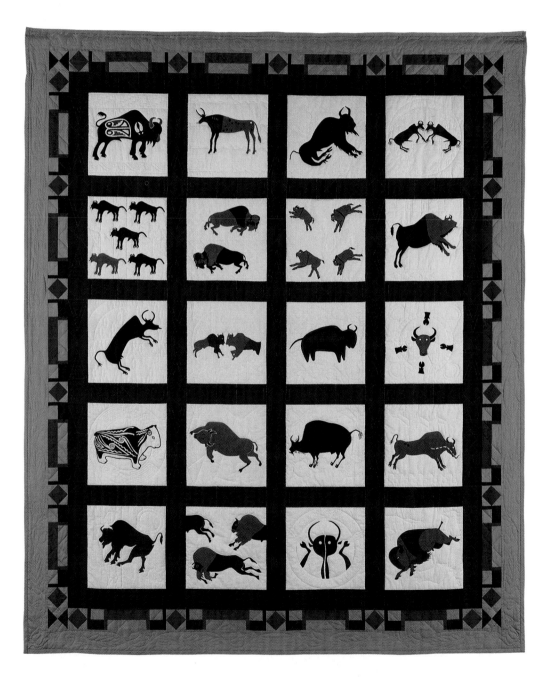

BUFFALO
MAGIC
75" x 90"
1984
Barbara
Pettinga Moore

Museum of AQS Collection

sometimes introduced as 'the lady who made the buffalo quilt.' Recognition, gallery showings and publication of this quilt gave me confidence.

Perhaps most gratifying was being asked by the editor of *Naturalist* magazine, who had seen the quilt on the cover of *Buffalo* magazine, to write an article about the Indian/bison history of the Plains. He wanted me to tie the quilt into the article, thereby integrating art and history. It worked!"

Linda Karel Sage
Morgantown, Indiana

Brown County Log Cabins

For BROWN COUNTY LOG CABINS, Linda Karel Sage used the Mountain Mist House Quilt pattern with her "own color variations." She comments, "My treatment was influenced by the area in which I live. Brown County, Indiana, is heavily wooded; the hilly countryside dotted by little log cabins. This beautiful place has been home to many artists since the early part of this century."

first place

1986 AQS Show & Contest Traditional Pieced, Ama

Linda continues, "The geometric quality of the blocks and lattice strips is softened by the wavy lines of the quilting. The border quilting echoes the little 'mountains' and rolling hills of Brown County, and the edging of 'pine-tree points' (a variation on Prairie Points I worked out) represents the deep green woods that surround us here in the county."

Speaking of her background, Linda says, "Born in Cedar Rapids, Iowa, of Welsh and Czech parents, I inherited a love of handiwork and fabrics. I was taught by my mother the skills of drawing,

sewing and knitting, and I still consider her my best art teacher. I studied art at the University of Iowa and received my B.A. in fine arts and M.A. in printmaking there. I began quilting in about 1980, and learned from other quilters I met, rather than from classes."

About BROWN COUNTY LOG CABINS, Linda says, "Although this is a pattern I purchased, I feel I made it my own work in the colors, fabrics, quilting and finishing details I used. Of all the quilts I have made, this one always gets the strongest response. I believe it is because people love the house pattern and thus get a cozy, warm feeling about the combined ideas of quilts and log cabins – so essentially American in quality. This quilt has appeared in

PHOTO: RICHARD SCHAFFNER

nine other shows, winning eight other awards. It has also been included in publications."

With respect to the effect of her award, Linda says, "The key word is 'validation.' When you win an award in a national competition, you add to the feeling of personal satisfaction in a piece well-designed and made, the knowledge that others acknowledge and appreciate the work you have done. For a woman, this is many times a new feeling. Of course, her family and friends appreciate her skills - but to some extent one expects to be supported by them. When strangers (and skilled ones) say: 'A job well done' - you just can't beat that for a great feeling! The fact that the monetary prizes are generous amounts backs up this approval and in a way brings one's skill into a position of value well above a 'hobby' designation. In very much the way Billie Jean King made women's tennis on par with men's tennis, AQS has made quilting a serious pursuit."

Linda's advice to other quiltmakers: "Imbue your work with as much of your own personality as you can. Forget about all the rules about what colors 'go

"If you enter a show, and don't win, that's disappointing to be sure, but remember this: those who do win validate the continuing pursuit of quilting excellence for us all."

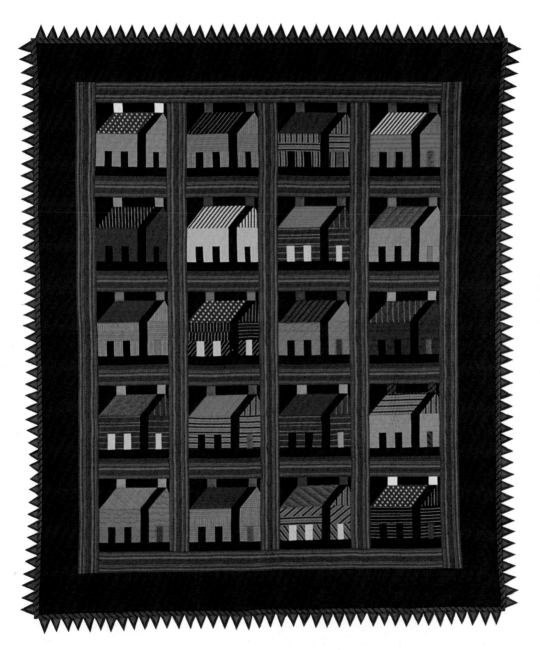

BROWN COUNTY
LOG CABINS
87" x 93"
1985
Linda Karel Sage

together' or what you have been taught about how you *must* do things. Enjoy yourself, make what you want, use the colors that you like, and work in the way that is most comfortable for you. See as many shows as you can, and look at quilts both old and new whenever you get a chance. Ask yourself what you like about a piece, and what, if anything, you would have done differently. Enter shows if you enjoy competing, and think carefully about the judges' written comments about your quilt."

Louise B. Stafford
Bremerton, Washington

Lincoln Quilt

The 3,325 squares in this quilt– 1¼" squares of blue, rose, pink, white and deep red prints featured on a white background with navy accents – were all scissors-cut, hand-pieced and hand-quilted!

Louise B. Stafford says that when she saw the cover quilt of the February 1982 *Quilter's Newsletter Magazine*, she knew that antique Lincoln

second place

1986 AQS Show & Contest Traditional Pieced, Ama

Quilt would be her challenge. She adds, "Small patchwork pieces are my favorite."

Born in quilting country on a Kansas farm in 1909, Louise later moved to Topeka, where her twin sister and she were educated and worked for Capper's Publishing Co. She continues, "We are both avid quilters. I moved to the Pacific Northwest in 1940, but did not start quilting again until 1974. Kansas and Washington, by phone, are a short but expensive distance apart for my sister and me to exchange

quilting ideas." Louise adds a note about another family collaboration, "An engineer husband is a very big plus for measurements and quilting designs."

Speaking of her award-winning quilt, Louise says, "This has always been one of my very favorites and is now hanging permanently in my home on a entrance-way wall. A husband and wife quilting couple from Seattle who saw

this quilt at the AQS show searched and located me so that they could make this Lincoln quilt." Louise adds, "A great, great granddaughter of Abraham Lincoln has said the original of this quilt was made by Lincoln's mother and her neighbor. It was started the year of his birth and quilted the following year."

Asked to give advice to other quiltmakers, Louise says, "Such wonderful friends

About placing in the AQS competition, Louise says, "I feel that this award has stimulated me to pursue the art of quilting to its fullest extent, and I now feel brave enough to tackle another one of my favorite quilts, the Baltimore Bride quilt."

LINCOLN QUILT
90" x 90"
1984
Louise B. Stafford

I have made in the quilting world far and near. I enjoy competition and probably do my very best in golf and quilting. These two hobbies keep me away from the rocking chair and gumming oatmeal."

Polly M. Sepulvado, MD
Roseburg, Oregon

Grandmother's Engagement Ring

Polly M. Sepulvado, MD says of her background, "I have always sewed. I knitted, crocheted, etc. In high school and college I made my clothes and my mom's because I liked to sew, plus we couldn't afford 'store bought' ones. I was exposed to quilts for the first time when I met Lucy Happ, a quilter from Oklahoma. I was a doctor and had joined the

third place

1986 AQS Show & Contest
Tradtional Pieced, Ama

Navy and Lucy was a career Navy nurse. I admired her quilts, bought some quilt books and taught myself to quilt."

She continues, "I made lots of mistakes and my first quilt stitches looked liked basting. Now I make three to four quilts per year and use a large frame that is always set up in the living room. I have a full-time practice of internal medicine, have children and am wife to a veterinarian. This proves that you can find time to do the things you want to do; it's the things you

don't want to do that you can't find time for – like dirty windows, etc. You've got to decide what's important."

Polly adds, "To me, quilting is VERY important. My quilts are not sacred. We sleep under them every

night, and I have quilts hanging in my waiting room that I rotate regularly. My patients seem to enjoy them a great deal."

Speaking of GRAND-MOTHER'S ENGAGEMENT RING, Polly explains, "The quilt was made from a Mountain Mist pattern for a Mountain Mist contest. Slides of the quilt were juried and it was *not* chosen to even be in the contest." Polly adds, "It was fun to make. My husband helped me choose which Mountain Mist pattern to make that would be a real show stopper."

Questioned about the effect of the AQS award, she

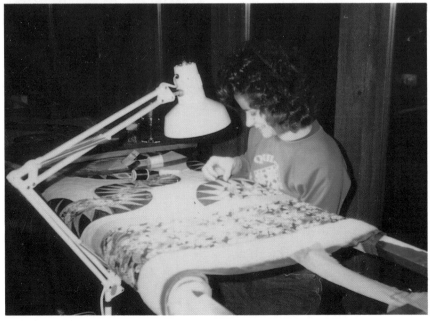

82

*Asked how she now feels about the quilt, Polly says, "I like the final effect.
Some quilts I make I think are nice but I don't necessarily LIKE.
This one I like – it makes me feel good about quilting."*

GRANDMOTHER'S
ENGAGEMENT
RING
76" x 94"
1986
Polly M.
Sepulvado, MD

Museum of AQS Collection

replies, "Winning has added VALUE to my passion. I appreciate what the American Quilter's Society and the Schroeder's have done for the quilter."

Her advice to other quilt-makers: "Quilting a little every day will finally produce a quilt."

Karin Matthiesen
Madison, Wisconsin

Bed Of Peonies

Speaking about this award-winning quilt, Karin Matthiesen says she developed it from a "traditional pattern from Mountain Mist." She was, in fact, making it for a contest sponsored by Mountain Mist – one which offered a wonderful cruise as the prize. The pattern she used was one she had had for some time and had always wanted to make. The

first place

*1986 AQS Show & Contest
Traditional Pieced, Pro*

pattern combines applique and pieced designs.

The quilt, with its 100% cotton batting, is quilted with feather circles and plumes. Looking at it now, she says, "It was worth every stitch I put into it." Karin says that the award the quilt won has given her "more confidence as a quiltmaker, and an appreciation of how much influence luck has on our lives."

Karin adds, "I was 32 years old when I made this quilt. I started quilting when I was 18 after seeing a quilt pattern in a magazine. I had sewn some clothing but that was my only experience at that time. I later took quilt classes from Klaudeen Hansen. I'm married, with two daughters, and I spend much of my time quilting."

Karin thinks her continued interest grows out of her love of the process of quiltmaking. And it is also the result of the fact that no matter how many quilts she makes there are always "hundreds more things" she would really love to do.

To other quiltmakers Karin says, "Design and make your quilts to please you – not what you think might please quilt contest judges."

BED OF
PEONIES
85" x 96"
1986
Karin
Matthiesen

Museum of AQS Collection

Aileen Stannis
Berkley, Michigan

Seven Sisters

Of her interest in quilt-making, Aileen Stannis says, "Sewing has always been an enjoyable part of my life, but after attending my first quilt show in 1976, sewing took over a greater part of each day. I took an all-day quilt class a month after that show, joined a quilt club and learned the art of quiltmaking and have enjoyed it ever since."

second place

1986 AQS Show & Contest Traditional Pieced, Pro

She continues, "I prefer traditional quilts with lots of quilting, both straight-line and fancy quilting. I draft all my patterns on graph paper and make templates from my drawings. I belong to a quilt club, Quaint Quilters, and am also a member of the Quilt Guild of Metro Detroit and a charter member of the Michi-gan Quilt Network."

About SEVEN SISTERS Aileen says, "This quilt consists of 28 groups of six-pointed stars – seven stars in each group to form a hexagon – set together with perfect triangles. The center stars are pieced from the same green fabric. Different prints are used for each of the remaining stars." Aileen adds, "This old traditional pattern is usually shown in darker colors, and each

group of stars is usually the same. Made of scraps of pastel prints, it makes a cheery quilt."

All fabrics used in this quilt are 100% cotton pastel prints and unbleached muslin. The quilt is hand-pieced and hand-quilted, and all stars are quilted ¼" from seams. Fancy Feather Quilting is used in the border.

Asked if she now feels any differently about this award-winning quilt, Aileen says, "No – It is still one of my favorite quilts." About the show experience she says, "I am very proud to have won an award in the AQS show. Having attended the show the last four years, I feel very privileged to have had a quilt in the 1986 show and in 1987 and 1989 shows also. Entering a competition is fun even if you do not win an award. Seeing other people enjoying your quilt is very rewarding."

"If it's worth making, it's worth making well. The hours I spend quilting are the most relaxing time of each day. I enjoy every minute."

SEVEN SISTERS
84" x 108"
1984
Aileen Stannis

Lois Tornquist Smith
Rockville, Maryland

Springtime Sampler

Lois Tornquist Smith's SPRINGTIME SAMPLER is a sampler quilt which incorporates blocks relating to springtime and family memories. Lois explains, "The Washington Monument is typical of my geographic area, Washington, D.C. Family pictures are incorporated in the Crazy Patch block. The Courthouse Steps block symbolizes my lawyer husband. Many of the

third place

1986 AQS Show & Contest Traditional Pieced, Pro

other blocks were just fun to do and I made them while teaching sampler classes in the area. (I find I am a much better teacher if I, too, am working on a quilt along with the students.)"

Lois is an NQA certified judge and teacher. Her classes have inspired many to quilt using innovative techniques with the sewing machine. She is the author of *Fun & Fancy: Machine Quiltmaking* (AQS). Commenting on her award-winning quilt, Lois says, "SPRINGTIME SAMPLER is one of my first quilts. It is pieced

and quilted entirely by machine. It was also my first effort with pastel colored fabrics. The unique setting of the blocks with the framed square on point was designed to take advantage of the striped fabric and has evoked much interest. Although it is not difficult to piece, each sashing section has 12 small pieces and is not recommended for anyone in a rush. The flowers in the centers of the large sashing blocks are stenciled and quilted."

About the quilt, Lois comments, "At the time I finished SPRINGTIME SAMPLER I felt it was my best effort. I had pieced with care and included a few original blocks. I was

pleased with the overall blending of color and design. Since 1986 I have made quilts with more texture. Each has had a definite theme which has required either research or introspection. I feel my more recent quilts contain a deeper sense of purpose. This does not diminish my feelings for this earlier quilt."

Speaking of her award, Lois says, "Upon hearing that I had won a ribbon in 1986, I called my husband at work. He said, "Well, I think we should go to Paducah for the Awards Banquet." I said, "Do you know how far that is? Eight hundred and fifty miles just for a dinner?" He seemed to sense more than I did the importance of winning. It was also the first tangible recognition or evidence that my husband thought 'my little hobby' was of any value. Since that time I have taught all over the country and met many wonderful quilters. The traveling and teaching have brought me much joy and satisfaction. I feel the win at Paducah had a lot to do with the wonderful things that have opened up for me in the quilting field."

Lois Smith's quilts have won many awards in addition to this AQS award, including

While in all quiltmaking we should strive for perfection, it is the process and the expression that has the greater value. Approach quiltmaking creatively. Don't be afraid to question and experiment. There is no right or wrong way. Whatever works for you should be YOUR WAY."

SPRINGTIME
SAMPLER
108" x 108"
©1986
Lois Tornquist
Smith

Museum of AQS Collection

Best of Show at Quilt Festival in Houston and several Blue Ribbons in National Quilting Association shows.

To other quiltmakers, Lois says, "Do your best without making it 'work.' Be flexible and patient. Time often gives insight and is a marvelous problem solver. Enjoy your designs and fabrics. Don't become discouraged when your piece takes an unexpected turn. Some of the most creative works are really surprises born out of frustration. Quiltmaking should be a pleasure and an outlet for artistic expression. If a person is able to view the world and translate its colors, scenes and experiences into fabric, they will, without a doubt, find much joy for themselves and for the viewing pleasure of others."

Nancy B. Clark
Phoenix, Arizona

Fugue

Nancy B. Clark writes, "FUGUE is machine-stitched and hand-quilted, with diagonal runs across the body. The batik-like fabric is combined with interlocking red and blue squares. The name FUGUE came as I was figuring how to put the parts together. The 200th birthday of J.S. Bach was being celebrated and, as I listened to a fugue, I thought how similar

first place

*1986 AQS Show & Contest
Innovative Pieced, Ama*

the construction of the two compositions were."

She continues speaking about the quilt, "The primary influence was the printed fabric. My two daughters and I all loved it, and I thought a quilt might be a way to share it, rather than to make a big skirt for one of us. The second influence was a friend who taught Creative Textiles at Arizona State University and was always inventing wonderful little and large pieces. The third influence was a friend who handed me an entry form for the 1985

AQS show with her assurance that my work should be made public."

"FUGUE," Nancy adds, "was my first quilt (the cross-stitch kit quilt that was so boring it took 30 years doesn't count). The picture of me working on my next quilt *(below)* shows a little mock-up that was the beginning of FUGUE. I had no idea of size of blocks, etc., and I keep that piece around because it cracks me up to think of doing a large quilt in such tiny pieces."

She discusses the competition, "Making this quilt brought together a love of color, design, and fabric in a

way that they could be in one whole, and be enjoyed in visual, tactile ways that feed the spirit. Entering the quilt meant I finished it and finished it well enough to please my own standards (which get pretty tough). Winning the Blue had the immediate effect of euphoria, a secondary effect of trying the next year, and a long-term effect of evaluating where my work fits into the competitive picture. At this point, I'm making quilts, but not directly for the fun of fame. The next quilt, "Phoenix Rising," won an honorable mention, a place in the AQS Engagement Calendar, and will live in the AQS museum."

Her advice to other quilt-makers: "Make quilts because you are driven to express something: a love of the way hues play with each other and variations of themselves, make one to celebrate, to mourn, to hope, to point a way. Make one to mark a new time in your life, to acknowledge a deep friendship. Pretend the fabrics are paint, and you are three years old, with the paint gushing through your fingers. Pretend

Looking back, Nancy comments, "At first I thought I should have given in and taken a series of courses for technique. Now I realize that I work best by myself, and take courses not for technique, but to see the connections between the artist and her or his work."

FUGUE
81" x 115"
1985
Nancy B. Clark

you are very old and wise and have a whole lot of good answers. I should just come out and say that women don't need any more stitch-counters evaluating their work and lives. But that's my bias and counter to why a lot of people stay in the quilting-for-competition world. If you are pleased with the results and want to share the beauty and magic, send it off somewhere so others with eyes to see...can."

Karmen Streng
Davis, California

Celebration Of Autumn

A floral centerpiece at a reception for a special California quiltmaker was the inspiration for Karmen Streng's CELEBRATION OF AUTUMN. The quilt was made of all-cotton fabric with polyester batting and was machine pieced and hand quilted. Karmen

second place

1986 AQS Show & Contest Innovative Pieced, Ama

reports, "The party was fun, and doing the quilt was an enjoyable challenge."

Describing her background and interests, Karmen writes, "I began sewing before junior high school. My original major at University of Utah was in a home economics field, though I finished with a B.S. in sociology and M.S.W. in social work. I still sew most of my own clothing including tailored

jackets. My first quilting class was in about 1976 after I was able to retire from being a social worker. I continue to take classes and enjoy participating in the world of quilting. I have two adult sons and a prince of a workaholic husband. He has one son, two daughters and one grandson. We enjoy baseball games and downhill skiing."

She continues, speaking especially to other quiltmakers, "The 'entering' is, for me, part of the process of quilting,

i.e. the completion of the quilt. Winning or doing well is the frosting. However, it took lots of entries for me to come to that realization. There can be only a few winners and each of us has to make our peace with that. If not winning is too painful, we have to find some other completion. I think it won't do to just say 'keep trying.' We need to know why we try so we can gain perspective and I think that that will be different for each quilter – probably for each quilt, too."

When asked about winning the AQS award, Karmen says,
"Doing well at something you enjoy is a wonderfully validating experience –
a real high! Entering subsequent shows and not winning or even placing
has made me appreciate even more how special that year was for me."

CELEBRATION
OF AUTUMN
86" x 86"
1985
Karmen Streng

Joan Ojerio
Kalamazoo, Michigan

Full Moon Rising

Joan Ojerio explains, "The pattern of this quilt is based upon four large Log Cabin blocks. I chose this pattern so that I could create the range of values seen in a moonlit sky. The triangles cutting through the blocks create a sense of radiating energy. One of the first quilt magazines I purchased featured Marie McCormick-Snyder and I was taken with her designs and use of color."

third place

1986 AQS Show & Contest Innovative Pieced, Ama

She continues, "All cotton materials, except polyester batting, were used in the construction. I machine and hand pieced and hand quilted. I made a template for each piece. This was before I knew of rotary cutters that would have made it easier to cut the long pieces. But I was very proud that this, my third quilt, came out very accurately made, exactly to the measurements of the scale drawing. Being a tool and die maker's daughter, this accuracy pleased me."

Of her background, Joan says, "At the time I made the quilt I had recently moved to Kalamazoo and finished taking my second quilting class, from Elaine Seaman who taught me the basics of good quilt design. I hold a degree in veterinary medicine, but I was not working at the time, having chosen to stay home with my four children. I was looking for something challenging to do, and an opportunity to be with other women, so I decided on quilting. I find I enjoy the creative process of quilting, and the friendships I have made with other quilters have been very important in my life."

About her quilt, Joan comments, "I hope that people who view my quilts find pleasure in the visual stimulation and are encouraged to make quilts of their own. I still find this quilt to be visually exciting and will some day make another like it, only not so large."

Of her show experience, Joan says, "The entry of the quilt and award at the AQS show was serendipitous. I would enjoy quilting whether I had won or not, but it was nice to receive an objective affirmation of my design abilities. This quilt also won a blue ribbon at the NQA show in 1986. Other people appreciated my ability and asked

"I think the large amount of noncompetitive sharing that goes on in guilds across the country is what has kept quiltmaking lively and growing."

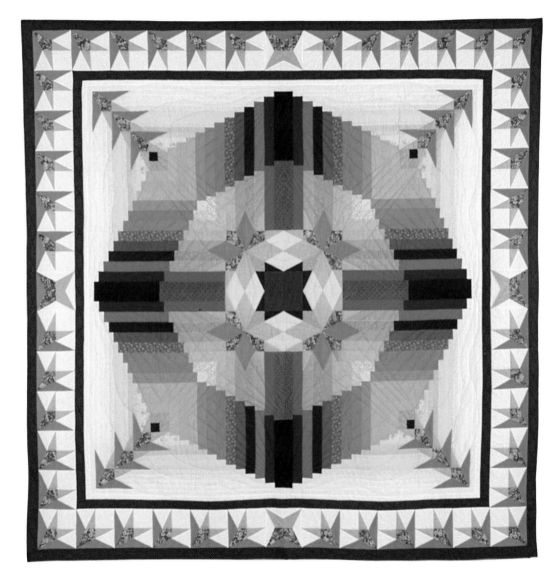

FULL MOON
RISING
108" x 108"
©1984
Joan Ojerio

me to teach. So I have taught classes that have mainly to do with use of color, and quilting design."

Speaking to other quilt-makers, Joan says, "Making quilts takes a big commitment of time. It is like gardening, or life itself – it takes many little tasks over a long period of time before you see the results. You have to be patient. If this is a process you enjoy, stick with it, the rewards will be there every day after it is complete when you see it on your wall, or use it on your bed or your child's bed. I don't make quilts for competitions. I find having to make a quilt to meet someone else's requirements to be inhibiting to my creative process. I like showing and sharing my quilts with others when they are done."

Moneca Calvert
Rocklin, California

Hearts

The original design for this award-winning quilt by native Californian Moneca Calvert uses three sizes of hearts set in two patterns that each repeat four times in an interlocking medallion. Over 40 fabrics were used to develop the quilt, ranging from pink through red, including peach, orange and purple to deep brownish rose. The quilt is machine-

first place

1986 AQS Show & Contest Innovative Pieced, Pro

pieced and hand-quilted with original designs.

About the quilt, Moneca says, "I created this piece specifically for the first AQS show in 1985. It was not completed in time. *Quilter's Newsletter Magazine* used it on the cover of the February 1986 issue, two weeks before I was honored with the grand prize for 'Glorious Lady Freedom' in the 1986

Great American Quilt Festival. I think I received more attention at the time from HEARTS' appearance on the cover!"

Moneca continues, "It is an extremely well known quilt and had won other awards before it was accepted at AQS in 1986. It appears in *America's Glorious Quilts* and has been a 10,000 copy commercial poster for an advertising

campaign. It is one of my most successful quilts!"

Of her background, Moneca says, "There were no quilts in my formative years. Largely self-taught, I have over 40 years sewing experience. In 1982 I 'discovered' the current quilting world! My first class from Katie Pasquini happened quite by chance and that led to the further discovery of related events such as shows, guilds, conferences and quilt publications and the knowledge that I, too, could be a part of it!"

She adds, "My preference leans towards curves and I have incorporated them in all my work whether it be clamshell, hearts, pictorials or whatever. I have received awards on all the quilts entered in competition and they are all special. I started teaching on a national level in 1985, and I am always aware of my good fortune to be actively creating and sharing QUILTS!"

"I knew from the beginning that it was a good design. I had no idea that it would force me to offer a workshop on the design technique. I have seen wonderful reproductions and variations come from this design technique which can be used with any geometrical form."

HEARTS
78" x 78"
1985
Moneca Calvert

Alison Goss
Hockessin, Delaware

Stravinsky's Rite

Alison Goss is "a self-taught quiltmaker with a varied background as a school teacher, environmentalist, production sewer, and wife and mother." She has been teaching quilting classes for ten years, and now travels nationwide to give workshops and lectures. Much of her work has "explored the use of strip piecing to translate themes from nature into

second place

1986 AQS Show & Contest Innovative Pieced, Pro

quilts"; she "concentrates on the use of color and design to create quilts which are visually exciting and challenging."

Speaking of the development of STRAVINSKY'S RITE, Alison says, "I used strip-piecing techniques adapted from my bargello quilts to interpret Stravinsky's music, 'The Rite of Spring.' I wanted to express the beauty and violence in the music, as well as its rhythmic complexity."

Continuing to describe the development of the quilt, Alison adds, "I made up nine

sets of strips, and 'composed' them on my studio wall, working from left to right. I hand quilted it in a free-form zigzag design inspired by stories of the dancers' confusion when they tried to perform during the riot provoked by the first performance of the music."

Asked what she would like people to know about the quilt, Alison replies, "My desire to interpret Stravinsky's music forced me to try

ideas I never would have thought of otherwise. I have found that music inspires my work on many levels."

About her AQS show experience, Alison comments, "When I won the award, Marty Bowne called to interview me; that was the first of several conversations that we had about music and quilts, leading to the Musical Medley shows at Quilting-By-the-Lake, as well as to my deepening interest in music. Mak-

"I was very excited about this quilt when I first made it, and I guess it is more of a 'comfortable companion' now. In my work, I try to recapture the excitement that I feel when I work hard to express ideas that are important to me, and the result is something new and surprising."

STRAVINSKY'S
RITE
76" x 60"
©1985
Alison Goss

ing this quilt has led me to explore the importance of music in my life, and while developing a workshop and lecture based on musical inspiration, I found that many quilters are profoundly influenced by music."

To other quiltmakers, Alison says: "Your quilts should be an expression of *yourself.* It is hard to be creative if you are worried about whether other people will like your quilt, or whether you have followed all the 'rules' correctly. If you have made your quilt to satisfy yourself, then it's wonderful if it wins an award in a competition, but you'll still love it even if it doesn't."

Marcia J. Lutz
Ball Ground, Georgia

Victorian Kaleidoscope

Marcia J. Lutz says VICTORIAN KALEIDOSCOPE "is an original design using ideas gathered from a Victorian stained-glass window book." She adds that she had also "been intrigued with using some Celtic quilting."

The quilt was hand-pieced, hand-quilted, and made of 100% cotton fabrics. Marcia comments, "My construction is the method of

third place

*1986 AQS Show & Contest
Innovative Pieced, Pro*

having the design drawn on paper, then tracing the pattern piece by means of a light box, adding the seam allowance and then sewing the pieces together. In order to get the correct angle for the kaleidoscope wedges, I used a large piece of paper and folded a circle into pie shapes. I then drew my design on one of the pie-shaped wedges, paying close attention to how the design would join the next wedge in the circle throughout the bands. (I use paper for all my quilting patterns and designs.)"

What Marcia would like others to know about VICTORIAN KALEIDOSCOPE is: "This quilt was a challenge in precision. A small variance could create havoc throughout the hundreds of pieces in the bands. The dark corners are pieced (except for the circles) and there are 55 different pattern pieces in each corner. The corners took 25 hours each to cut and piece. In all, the quilt took approximately 1,000 hours to complete." Speaking of her show experience, Marcia says,

"Because I was a winner at AQS, I feel I've been invited to exhibit my quilts at other national shows from Stone Ridge, New York, to the West Coast Quilter's Conference in Sacramento, California. I've felt proud to know something I enjoy doing measures up in competition, and it pleases me to know others have enjoyed seeing my quilts in shows."

To other quiltmakers, Marcia suggests: "Always give a project your best effort. Enter all the competitions

"This quilt made me feel I could do any design I could create. The obstacle would be finding the hours required for completion."

VICTORIAN
KALEIDOSCOPE
80½" x 80½"
1986
Marcia J. Lutz

VICTORIAN KALEIDOSCOPE also won the Viewer's Choice Award.

you desire and know that if you don't win, you have contributed to the 'symphony' of the show and given others the pleasure of seeing your creative efforts. Above all, enjoy every moment spent making your quilt – 'this is your life – it's not a dress rehearsal,' as someone once said."

Josephine Royer
Thurmont, Maryland

Keepsake Quilt

Josephine Royer explains that KEEPSAKE QUILT is based on a 1971 pattern published by the Hearst Corporation, in *Good Housekeeping Needlecraft*. Josephine says she "used the pattern given except for stuffing some of the flowers and eliminating the yo-yos." She adds that

first place

1986 AQS Show & Contest
Applique, Amateur

the quilt is constructed of "mostly cotton" and she used "basic construction and quilting" to complete the quilt.

About her background, Josephine says, "In 1968, I decided to make a quilt for each of our three daughters. At that time, quilting information was 'few and far between.' By trial and error I completed an Eight-Pointed Star quilt and a Lone Star quilt. It was then time to begin our youngest daughter Jamie's quilt. Jamie was eight years old at the time. To my surprise she had chosen her quilt from the one small quilt booklet I had been using. It was an applique, the Bluebell. Upon finishing it, five years later, Jamie remarked, 'Mom, I thought you would die before finishing mine.' Since then, applique has been my favorite."

Asked what she would most like people to know about her KEEPSAKE QUILT, Josephine replies, "This, to me, was an example of what you can accomplish if you really put your mind to it and want to." She adds, "It just amazes me that I really made it."

Speaking of her first place award at the 1986 AQS show, Josephine comments, "It has given me more confidence in myself."

"Have confidence in yourself and your work. Keep competing and striving to do your best and you will. It may not be the blue ribbon but you've used all the talent God gave you and you cannot ask for more than that."

KEEPSAKE QUILT
95" x 95"
1985
Josephine Royer

Doris Amiss Rabey
Hyattsville, Maryland

President's Wreath Variation

Doris Amiss Rabey joined the National Quilting Association in 1973 "to learn to quilt two inherited tops." About the development of PRESIDENT'S WREATH VARIATION she says, "I had liked the President's Wreath design after first seeing it in a magazine. I clipped out the picture and pattern and sometime later when I decided to make this quilt, found the

second place

1986 AQS Show & Contest Applique, Amateur

pattern incorrect, necessitating my redesigning my square to fit. I felt my original-design border and sashing also worked well."

Cotton and blends were used for the design, which is hand-appliqued and hand-quilted. "The blocks are machine stitched together.

The main blocks are stipple quilted for added dimension and contrast."

Speaking of her work, Doris says, "My husband, Jim, is a great helper; he cuts all my applique pieces and helps draft my patterns, critiques my work and takes me to quilt shows."

Doris feels this quilt is an example of how quilters can meet the challenging problems works sometimes pose. She says, "Do not despair when things do not work out – redesign, change fabrics and colors and go on. Try new settings, sashings, borders and see what develops. Mine often do not work to my

satisfaction but this one pleased me very much. I hope others also enjoy it."

Of her feelings about this quilt, Doris says, "I liked it then, I like it now. I know how dejected I was at first when my pattern did not fit my block properly but I improvised and all turned out well I thought. I was most pleased, even more so after winning the award at AQS." Her advice for other quiltmakers: "Everyone has to start somewhere. With practice, improvement is bound to follow. Make your quilt, enjoy it and do enter competitions so others may also enjoy it."

"The winning quilts' being shown in American Quilter *magazine spreads the show to many who were not able to attend in person. I heard from a number of old friends, plus some new ones offering congratulations. That was a pleasant surprise."*

PRESIDENT'S
WREATH
VARIATION
72" x 96"
1986
Doris Amiss
Rabey

Museum of AQS Collection

Maxine Bossing
Springfield, Missouri

Folk Art Medallion

What Maxine Bossing would most like people to know about FOLK ART MEDALLION is that it was her own idea, and it was all done by hand – the quilting, applique, embroidery and stuffing. She adds that it took almost 400 hours to quilt.

Speaking of the development of the design, Maxine says, "I had taken a tole painting class, doing tulips

third place

1986 AQS Show & Contest
Applique, Amateur

and hearts, so I just combined the patterns, making the size I wanted for the center." She continues, "I had bought four yards of pretty border print, not knowing what I wanted to do with it. After designing the center, I bought fabric matching the colors from the border print. I'm not an artist, so I didn't have in mind what I wanted

to do next. (Which is not a good idea.) It took me quite a while to decide. After I got the whole quilt finished, I decided to add a little extra touch by stuffing all the hearts and tulips. (I just took out a few of the applique stitches, stuffed it a little and then re-appliqued that part.)"

About her background, Maxine says, "I am 62 years old now. I started quilting 10 years ago. I have always enjoyed sewing, but never did think I wanted to learn to

quilt. Then I saw a beautiful white whole-cloth quilt and decided to try. I loved it and my only regret is 'Why didn't I start when I was younger!' I have a son and daughter and two granddaughters. I want to pass my quilts on down to them." She adds, "I have written poems about some of my quilts to make them more meaningful to whoever receives them. My husband is a good supporter of my work and enjoys showing off my quilts to friends."

Of her AQS experience, Maxine says, "I was very happy to win the award. It was encouraging and made me want to do something more challenging."

Asked to provide advice for other quiltmakers, Maxine suggests, "Don't get discouraged if you make a mistake. Just keep trying; each time will get better." She adds that it is "best to have the complete design in your mind and on paper before starting."

"I have made lots of new friends. Someone will ask
'May I bring a friend or relative over to see your quilts?'
And I'm always glad to show them."

FOLK ART
MEDALLION
74" x 95"
1985
Maxine Bossing

Anne J. Oliver
Alexandria, Virginia

Four Seasons Album

Anne J. Oliver explains, "This quilt evolved when I decided that I didn't want to copy the Baltimore Album, but rather create one of my own from my time. Original patterns depict my life in twenty blocks, using the Baltimore Album style of applique in shapes and color combinations."

Speaking of the development of the quilt, Anne says,

first place

1986 AQS Show & Contest Applique, Professional

"100% cotton was used. All appliques were made with my freezer paper method, created in early 1980's. Quilting designs were also created with folded freezer paper and free-handed too. Names of children, words, etc. are scripted into the background along with loose meandering, generally hidden."

Anne says she began quilting in 1975, making "every mistake in the books," but finished her first quilt and "became addicted." When her children began to grow up, she chose lecturing and

giving workshops over a full-time job. She refers to herself as a frustrated oil painter and watercolorist, explaining, "Quilting became my expression of my love for art. I have published many articles, and am now interested in presenting architectural motifs in my quilts, bringing back the metal ceiling era at the turn of the century."

Asked what she would most like people to know about FOUR SEASONS ALBUM, Anne replies, "It is a true expression of my desire to create and balance, but I used the security of the Baltimore Album colors, which made

Photo courtesy of Continental Quilting Congress

putting the quilt together easy. It was the most fun of all the work I have done, most personalized, most loved by the public, except the men love *Painted Metal Ceiling*. FOUR SEASONS ALBUM showed how much leeway a quilter has in the appliques and the quilting, and folding freezer paper was the tool that made it easy, easy, easy."

In response to questions about her current feelings for the quilt, Anne says, "It is the one quilt that I could not part with, no matter what was offered. It should be in a museum rather than being handed down to the family because it depicts the joy that I think the ladies that made the Baltimore Albums must have had when they created their masterpieces. It is a tribute to their talents. I'm glad I created my own rather than trying to duplicate their quilts."

Speaking of her award, Anne explains, "Awards give me the incentive to finish my work (I am a procrastinator), they allow many people to see my work, so I can teach through publications and

"PLEASE take the words I CAN'T out of your vocabulary. Creativity isn't dead; it's just waiting for the bold quilters to attack it. Make loads of mistakes, but win in the end. It's easy. And feel that YOU ARE GOOD."

FOUR SEASONS
ALBUM
80" x 96"
1984
Anne J. Oliver

visuality, and they give me the boost that I need many times – that my work with the use of freezer paper can compete with the best of the quilts. I need tools to make my quilting easier, or I will give up easily."

Linda Goodmon Emery
Derby, Kansas

Rosemaling Inspiration

Linda Goodmon Emery says about ROSEMALING INSPIRATION, "This original design was based on the rosemaling painting technique. I was inspired to try this technique after seeing a crib quilt made by Helen Kelley. I met Helen Kelley very briefly and expressed my desire to make this kind of quilt and mentioned I would like to take her class on it. It was not pos-

second place

1986 AQS Show & Contest
Applique, Professional

sible for me to take the class, but she encouraged me to try it anyway."

The quilt is made of cotton fabrics in clear, solid colors with flexible ribbon floss embellishment, and is hand-appliqued and hand-quilted. Linda comments, "This quilt was made for the specific purpose of entering it in this show. I really didn't have much time as the quilt was no more than an idea the August before the spring 1986 show. So I worked 52 hours a week for 6½ months

to finish it in time. It was good discipline. The quilt turned out far better that I had hoped (which is not always the case)."

She continues, "Obtaining the clear, bright colors I wanted to use was a challenge when nearly everything was being made in the soft, grayed-down colors then. The red fabric, for example, took me a couple of weeks, visits to countless quilt shops and fabric stores and probably 400 miles of driving."

Of her background, Linda says, "I have been a quilter since 1975 and specialize in original-design quilts of all

sizes and techniques. During my husband's Air Force career, we lived on both coasts, in the Midwest and overseas. Our three children are grown and we have three grandchildren."

Linda is author of *A Treasury of Quilting Designs* (AQS), is a National Quilting Association Master Quilter, and has won awards in numerous quilting shows. She also teaches, lectures and designs patterns. Her quilts have been featured in several quilt magazines and books.

Speaking of her 1986 AQS show experience she says, "This was the first time I had entered a national quilt show and was overwhelmed at winning. It has gained me recognition and a desire to keep trying to stretch my limits as a quiltmaker. (My family and friends were not surprised at my winning but I certainly was!)"

To other quiltmakers she says: "Winning is not the most important thing – the trying, growth and knowledge you gain is invaluable. If you keep 'hanging in there' you can't help but improve."

*"Don't ever be intimidated by another quiltmaker's quilts.
Set your goals high and keep pushing to reach them –
you just never know what you are capable of achieving unless you try."*

ROSEMALING
INSPIRATION
81" x 95"
©1986
Linda Goodmon
Emery

Museum of AQS Collection

Anita Shackelford
Bucyrus, Ohio

Baltimore Bride's Quilt

Anita Shackelford's BALTI-MORE BRIDE'S QUILT was made from a pattern by Patricia Cox. "I have always loved applique, and I think of this quilt as the beginning of my 'serious' work. I thought when I started this quilt that it would be the ultimate challenge to my skills and my patience. I worked on it off and on for two years. I learned a lot about layered

third place

1986 AQS Show & Contest Applique, Professional

applique and embellishment. Although I was working with a pattern, I began to add subtle changes to make it my own. I am still challenged by intricate applique, but have begun to design my own patterns, adding dimensional techniques and personal motifs. I feel that creating my own designs has taken my work to another level."

The quilt is hand appliqued and hand quilted and contains a small amount of embroidery, stuffed work, trapunto and stipple quilting. Anita adds, "The first time

that this quilt was shown in competition was in Paducah. To win there was a high point in my life, and gave me confidence to keep working and challenging myself. I have since had many ribbons on this and other quilts."

About her background, Anita explains, "I have been making quilts since 1967 and have been teaching quiltmaking for 10 years. I have taught in shops, for guilds, for adult education and privately in my home. I also enjoy studying antique quilts and am interested in documentation and conservation. I have been a member of NQA since 1982 and am currently

serving on the board as membership chairman. I am a charter member of AQS and also a member of the American Quilt Study Group." Anita's work has been included in several invitational exhibits and in *American Quilter* and *Quilter's Newsletter Magazine.*

Anita continues, "On the personal side, I have a husband, Richard and daughters, Jennifer, 20 and Elisa, 18. Dick and I both grew up in Bucyrus, but we have also lived in Columbus, Ohio, while he was in college, plus Florida and Puerto Rico, while he was in the Navy. I am a registered nurse and work part time in obstetrics. I enjoy aerobics and cooking and our family activities include gardening and sailing."

About her working style, Anita says, "I work on several quilts at a time and try to finish one or two a year, although some of them have taken almost three years to complete. Although I began quilting on a purely practical level (making bed quilts), quilting has become an artistic outlet for me. I seem to have this 'need' to create, and

"BALTIMORE BRIDE'S QUILT is an updated version of the applique album quilts made c.1840 in the Baltimore area. I think that these quilts were the ultimate in style and workmanship and I was excited and challenged by this pattern."

BALTIMORE
BRIDE'S QUILT
85" x 97"
1986
Anita
Shackelford

I love the medium of fabric. I also enjoy teaching and seeing students get 'turned on' to this art. But the best part of quilting is really the people. High on the list at every quilt show or event is the opportunity to visit with friends from past shows and to meet new ones."

June Culvey
Garden Prairie, Illinois

An Amish Nod

June Culvey explains that the Amish girls on this quilt were adapted from a Hastings cross-stitch book, and the setting and the pieced block were her own design. She adds, "Janice Streeter's crisp folded triangles on trees prompted the folded nosegay block of mine."

About the quilt, June says, "I wanted to make a cute, truly different kind of

first place

1986 AQS Show & Contest Other Techniques, Ama

Amish quilt. My husband Daniel made the templates for the quilt blocks as he does for all my quilts. We have a home among the

Amish in Mattoon, Kentucky and the little girls are so cute that I thought a cute Amish quilt was in order."

In response to a question about whether her feelings for the quilt are different now than when she made it, June says, "Yes, it was difficult for

me to work on an all solid quilt – with no calico to spark it up. I didn't care for it very much when it was done. It used to be the last quilt I would take out of the chest to air out. Now I see it as a lesson in color discipline. Working with colors you thought you didn't like can produce the opposite effect. I now treat this quilt with as much respect as the others."

About her AQS show experience, June comments, "I am a housewife and mother. While these two occupations are my primary motives in life, I needed something just for me to do. Quilting has filled that area. AQS has given that area a validity. Winning always produces a shot of much needed self-esteem."

"Take your time and do the best job you can with the knowledge you have. Be prepared to really work at it because rarely have I seen an 'overnight' sensation make it to the finals."

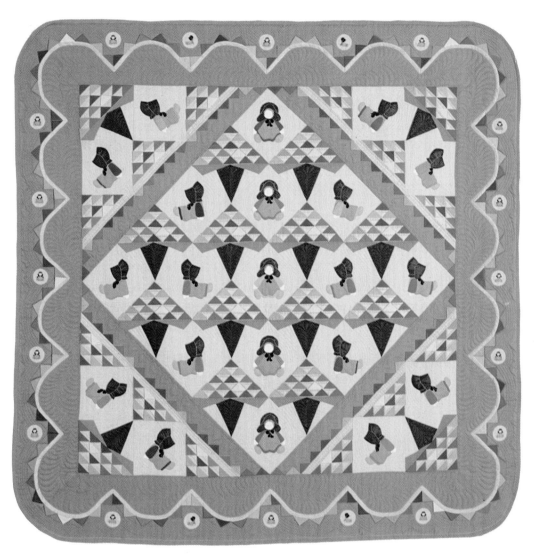

AN AMISH NOD
72" x 72"
1986
June Culvey

Patricia K. Spadaro
Delmar, New York

Quilted Counterpane

Patricia K. Spadaro tells us that when she began this quilt she "wanted to use an all-over design to complete a whole-cloth quilt." She adds, "The pattern used was an old Mountain Mist pattern entitled Quilted Counterpane."

She used a Dusty Rose polished cotton and marked the design using a light box she made from cardboard boxes, glass, and a gooseneck

second place

*1986 AQS Show & Contest
Other Techniques, Ama*

lamp. The markings were made with washable pen and she then quilted the lines using a polycotton blend thread she had heat-coated with melted parafin. She tells us, "This whole-cloth quilt has hand quilting every half inch, approximately 14 stitches to the inch," and adds that all this stitching was accomplished "without the use of a thimble!"

About her background, Patricia writes, "After growing up on the West Point, New York, military post, I pursued a fashion career. I worked for the Simplicity Pattern Company in New York City. I became interested in quilting in 1978 and have made approximately 20 quilts. I am presently married and have two grown daughters and show Labrador Retrievers as a hobby. QUILTED COUNTERPANE was my first contest quilt."

Patricia tells us this quilt was made especially for the 1985 AQS Show. Of her quilt's success she says, "I am proud the quilt was accepted into the show, won a prize and was purchased by AQS."

She continues, "At the time I received local newspaper and TV coverage. Many quilters called me and asked questions about entering contests. Entering the competition gave me the impetus to continue making quality quilts and to encourage others."

"While making quilts for competition, I would advise quiltmakers to take the time to insure accuracy in designing, marking, stitching and quilting. Then, TAKE GOOD SLIDES!"

QUILTED
COUNTERPANE
72" x 102"
©1985
Patricia K.
Spadaro

Museum of AQS Collection

Bonnie K. Browning
Greenwood, Indiana

A Little Bit Of Candlewicking

Bonnie Kay Kirkland Browning was born and raised in Muscatine, Iowa. She writes, "My mother taught me to sew as a young girl. I worked fifteen years as an executive secretary, which taught me patience, precision and organization – all qualities especially helpful in quilting. I made my first quilt in 1979 and by the early 1980's was being asked to

third place

*1986 AQS Show & Contest
Other Techniques, Ama*

teach through local adult education programs and art centers. My quilts have won numerous awards at local, regional and national quilt shows. I am extremely proud to have my quilt, A LITTLE BIT OF CANDLEWICKING, included in the AQS museum; and two of my quilts, WIND TRADE TULIPS and LACE REVIVAL, are in the Artists of Iowa Collection at the First National Bank of Waterloo, Iowa."

Bonnie says she has always been very active in quilting groups, and adds

that she and her husband currently live in Greenwood, Indiana. "He is in management with the J.C. Penney Company and therefore transfers from one location to another." Bonnie credits her quilting and quilting friends with making these moves easier – "quilters talk a universal language!"

A LITTLE BIT OF CANDLEWICKING "is made up of twelve 11½ inch candlewicked blocks of traditional quilt patterns. Sashing strips are covered entirely with Cluny lace with satin ribbon added to give that old-time elegance of yesterday's 'best' quilts. Borders feature a quilted rose defined by sculpture-like quilting lines." The quilt is constructed of 100% cotton permanent press unbleached muslin. Also

incorporated were 42 yards of lace and ribbon: 7 yards gathered ecru Cluny lace, 17½ yards cotton Cluny insertion lace and 17½ yards satin ribbon (inserted in Cluny lace). Bonnie worked on the quilt from February-December, 1983; nearly 400 hours of quilting time were involved.

Speaking of the quilt, Bonnie comments, "It is my most favorite quilt that I've made. There is something about the understated elegance of all-white quilts that makes them special. The size of this quilt is unusual because it was made especially to fit an antique spool bed."

Bonnie says she is "particularly interested in those types of quilts that have survived in fewer numbers, such as candlewicked, stenciled and whole-cloth quilts."

About her show experience, Bonnie says the 1986 AQS show was her first experience entering a national quilt competition. She adds, "It was a great confidence builder to me to know that my work was of the calibre to win an award at this level. I was thrilled just to have my quilt juried into the AQS show."

"As a quilt judge, certified by the NQA, I see a continual improvement in our quiltmaking. Most of this improvement, I think, is because many of our shows are judged shows. Entering a quilt in a judged competition is the cheapest quilt lesson a quilter can get. And, if your quilt wins an award, money or ribbon, that's just the icing on the cake!"

A LITTLE BIT OF
CANDLEWICKING
64" x 96"
1983
Bonnie K.
Browning

Museum of AQS Collection

Annabel Baugher
Galt, Missouri

Hanging Garden

Annabel Baugher says that this whole-cloth quilt is "an exact duplicate of a pattern published by the Stearns and Foster Co." To construct the quilt, Annabel used 50% cotton-polyester sheets. She explains, "Though it is reversible, the side most considered as the top is a percale sheet and the bottom is a muslin sheet. The muslin sheet was used for the back because it is more loosely woven and of coarser

first place

1986 AQS Show & Contest
Other Techniques, Pro

threads, thus making the planned trapunto easier. All marking, quilting and trapunto was done on the muslin side of the quilt. By using yarn and small strips of batting threaded in a tapestry needle to do the trapunto the fabric was not damaged in any way and the quilt is really reversible."

About her experiences with the quilt, Annabel comments, "This is the only quilt I have made just for a judge's eyes, and it will be the last! I started it for a Stearns and Foster Co. contest. When the due date arrived, the quilt was not even half done. Once you, or at least I, have ventured into creating my own designs, following a pattern completely with no deviation is no fun and very little challenge. It being my first experience with trapunto on a large piece was my only challenge. Yes it turned out well, and yes it is very pretty."

Speaking of her background, Annabel says, "I did not grow up in a family of quilters, but a family who appreciated and practiced excellent hand sewing." She explains that once she began quilting, "a real love" quickly developed, particularly for detailed whole-cloth quilts. Annabel makes quilts as expressions of love for her family, and hopes to leave a legacy of finely-crafted quilts for future generations.

*"It is always a joy to receive an award for a quilt I have made.
When people in the area where we live bring their visiting friends
and relatives from other states and yes even other nations
it gives me the mixed feeling of joy, humility and pride."*

HANGING GARDEN
78" x 88"
1986
Annabel Baugher

Rumi O'Brien
Middleton, Wisconsin

A Man's Life

About the development of A MAN'S LIFE, Rumi says, "The tedium of doing dishes one night inspired me to make this quilt." Rumi doesn't like to own many things, so she has no dishwasher. She finds that, like dishwashing, much of life is a repetition. As she was doing the dishes, she thought, "How can I get something from this dishwashing." Then she decided "to make

second place

*1986 AQS Show & Contest
Other Techniques, Pro*

this into a quilt." She explains, "A MAN'S LIFE is a repetition – small chores have to be done for tomorrow to go on smoothly."

Rumi was born in Tokyo, Japan and attended John Herron Art School in Indianapolis from 1959 through 1962. She has been a homemaker ever since. Rumi explains that she is very domestic, and that's how the quilting entered into her life. She cut up fabrics for

dresses and saved the scraps, and liked the idea of using them in quilts. She says that before quilting was popular she took a class in a local shop and made a sampler.

Her second quilt won an award in the 1985 show, and this is her third. She comments that she did not know very much about quilting when making even this quilt. She quilted it without a thimble and actually wore away half of one of her fingernails. She says, "While working one day I noticed I was making

faces while quilting, and I thought that some day I would use these expressions in a quilt. I went to the mirror many times to look at my expression. My next quilt, "Quilting Bees," used that idea. All over it quilters are shown resting on needles, grimacing, having a cup of tea – doing all the things we do when quilting" (detail shown below).

Rumi's aim is to make one quilt each year, but she says other activities and projects often keep her from completing the works on schedule.

"Don't lose the spirit women put into quilts when quilting was a necessary activity using scraps."

A MAN'S LIFE
63" x 83"
1986
Rumi O'Brien

Marian Shenk
Scottdale, Pennsylvania

Shadow Baltimore Bride

About her award-winning quilt SHADOW BALTIMORE BRIDE, Marian Shenk says, "I had no pattern. When I started I didn't know what the end result would be. I did all the blocks first and then made a center section to fit them. I cut squares of fabrics and folded them in different ways and cut out my flowers and leaves." Speaking of her use of shadow applique she

third place

1986 AQS Show & Contest Other Techniques, Pro

says, "It is an alternative to an applique quilt (but looks like applique) for those who haven't mastered the art of applique. I feel I can get more detailed with this method than I can with applique."

Describing the quilt's development, Marian explains, "I made each block different, using brightly colored cotton broadcloth for the designs. I laid them on an off-white background with a layer of voile over them. Then, using two strands of embroidery floss in a brighter color, I quilted the pieces in

between the two layers. When all sections were finished I sewed them together, added borders, marked the designs and quilted it again. This gives a very soft elegant look. She continues, "I have since made more of this type quilt and not one is the same and I feel my later ones are more attractive than the one in the show. I have gotten more detailed and intricate in my designs – also more varied with the kinds of materials used."

Of her background, Marian says, "I am married 38 years to a wonderful husband who is supportive of my quilt-

ing habit. He is quite verbal in talking about some of my creations to our friends, not short of bragging. We have one daughter and two sons and five grandchildren, who will all eventually have one of my creations. As I was growing up I was quite happy with a piece of fabric and needle and thread. My mother and grandmother all sewed and made quilts, so I grew up with this type of influence."

Marian continues, "After all the children left home I opened up a fabric and quilt shop in our town. I was making so many things my husband decided I needed an outlet for them before he was consumed by them. After being a busy mother and housewife for years, the shop gives me a whole new way of spending my time and I really enjoy every moment of it."

Of her AQS show experience, Marian says, "It has given me more confidence in my creative abilities. I find myself constantly trying to come up with something more beautiful and exciting. I tend to be very traditional and am finding it more difficult to compete with the more con-

"I was influenced by the Baltimore Album quilts but didn't like all the harsh bright colors used in them, so I came up with the idea to tone it down and make it more appealing to me."

SHADOW
BALTIMORE
BRIDE
86" x 102"
1985
Marian Shenk

Museum of AQS Collection

temporary types of quilts that are winning these days; that's not my style."

Her advice to other quilt-makers: "Never give up. Keep trying. I never expected to win with this quilt. I was very happy my quilt was accepted in this very prestigious quilt show and contest. Winning was an extra bonus."

Miriam Nathan-Roberts
Berkeley, California

The Worms Crawl In, The Worms Crawl Out

Miriam Nathan-Roberts says THE WORMS CRAWL IN, THE WORMS CRAWL OUT is another quilt in her interweave series which includes her 1985 award-winning quilt *Lattice Interweave*. Like that quilt, this one was hand-quilted by Sarah Hershberger.

Miriam designed her own pattern and hand dyed and hand painted the fabric for THE WORMS CRAWL IN, THE WORMS CRAWL OUT. She says

first place

1986 AQS Show & Contest Team Quilt

about the development of the quilt, "In this piece I wanted to see how the grid looked as it changed size and density. I also wanted to contrast its severe structure to the randomness of the worms. I wanted to see the play between the structure and playfulness."

Asked how she feels about the quilt now, Miriam comments, "I always like the quilt I finished most recently best." Miriam tends to work on two series at once, usually "breaking out of" one in order to work with the other. Currently she is working with the interweave series which is very "controlled and intellectual" and an architectural series which involves "wild fabrics" and "little planning." She adds, "I thought I was finished with the interweave series, but another quilt demanded my attention. I have just finished it."

Miriam holds a B.S. in home economics from Cornell University, with a concentration in clothing and design, and an M.A. in educational psychology from University of California, Berkeley. She teaches special education, job sharing with another teacher. Her quilts have been included in many exhibitions and she has been winning awards for her work since 1980.

Talking of her background, she says she had her first child at 40, a son who is now eight years old. It made her feel as if it were time to either "fish or cut bait." She decided at that time that she was going to make "her own quilts" from then on.

About winning the AQS award, Miriam says, "It has helped me to take my quilt-making seriously – it really helps my family to take my quiltmaking seriously."

"There should be communication between you and the piece you're working on. It's hard to be open, to not let a fixed idea get in the way. Let your work speak to you."

THE WORMS
CRAWL IN,
THE WORMS
CRAWL OUT
100" x 100"
1986
Miriam
Nathan-Roberts

Quilted by
Sarah
Hershberger

Sandra Heyman, Burns, Kansas
Linda Nonken, El Dorado, Kansas

San Lin Roses

Sandra Heyman and Linda Nonken began working together as quiltmakers in 1983. Together, they have constructed eleven major quilts, two of which have been Sweepstakes winners at the Kansas State Fair (1984 and 1986). They have also won ribbons and Viewer's Choice awards at many other judged shows, and their quilts have been featured in

second place

1986 AQS Show & Contest Team Quilt

various quilting magazines and calendars.

Sandra is a master wheat weaver and since 1976 has been an exhibitor at War Eagle Farm in Arkansas. Linda has done alterations professionally since 1977 and is currently producing a line of folk jewelry and dolls. Sandra is making miniature quilts from feed sacks. Both

have done needlework and sewing since early childhood. This shared effort began on a shopping trip in 1983. Sandra mentioned an antique bed for which she wanted a quilt. Linda said, "I'll help you...," and the partnership began. Linda lives near El Dorado, Kansas, and Sandra lives near Burns, Kansas, and their families have been friends for many years.

The original design for SAN LIN ROSES was developed on hexagon graph paper. The ¾" hexagons were appliqued and pieced utilizing purchased fabrics and the English piecing method.

Sandra Heyman (left) and Linda Nonken

Sandra and Linda comment on the "influence of antique Victorian watercolor paintings of rose studies" on the design. They add, "We usually hand quilt in hoops on one of our round oak tables (photo below). However, SAN LIN ROSES was quilted in a standing frame."

Speaking of this AQS award, Sandra and Linda explain that winning the award has had an important effect on their lives. "It has validated our time and energy. It is encouraging to win considering how many people were competing."

To other quiltmakers, Sandra and Linda recommend: "Do your very best on each quilt because you may want to enter a contest with it some day. You refine and hone your work on each of your quilts if you make them for competition. There is always a place for each quilt in a show somewhere. Don't give up with one rejection."

"The SAN LIN ROSES quilt seemed like our rite of passage – from casual quiltmakers to serious quiltmaking partners."

SAN LIN
ROSES
60" x 80"
©1985
Sandra Heyman
Linda Nonken

Sharon Heidingsfelder
Little Rock, Arkansas

Parallel Melody

This award-winning quilt's original design by Sharon Heidingsfelder involved a repeated block pattern. Sharon constructed the quilt of 100% cotton fabric, designed the quilting, and then arranged to have Mrs. Jonas Raber of Millersburg, Ohio, execute the hand quilting.

Speaking of the quilt, Sharon says, "I never wanted

third place

1986 AQS Show & Contest Team Quilt

to make quilts because I was 'afraid' of all the technical aspects of them. This quilt confirmed that a quilt is not that hard to make – just time-consuming, for which I'd gladly give all my time.

Sharon holds a B.S. in interior design from The Pennsylvania State University and an M.S. in crafts from the University of Tennessee. She presently works as a crafts specialist with the University of Arkansas Cooperative Extension Service.

When asked why she quilts, Sharon speaks of the "pleasures of combining colors and patterns." Before becoming involved in quilting, she had worked in ceramics and then silk screening. She says she made her first quilt because she wanted a quilt and "didn't want to pay someone to make it." She took a class

with Nancy Crow, who helped her determine the direction in which she should go. Then Sharon made her first quilt, which was accepted in Quilt National! PARALLEL MELODY was her third. She says she keeps going because "there are always fabrics left over. This leads to the next quilt, the development of which always necessitates buying more fabric. It's never ending."

One of the things Sharon likes about quilting is that everything is "up front." "Unlike with ceramics, where one never knows exactly what will come out of the kiln and one's entire project can be destroyed when a pot cracks, with quilting one knows exactly what the finished product will be and has the option of changing that if it doesn't seem right."

Sharon's advice to other quiltmakers: "Never give up.
Enter as many competitions as possible.
Also enter your quilts in non-quilt-related shows.
This will help elevate quilts to the art form that they are."

PARALLEL MELODY
72" x 72"
©1985
Sharon
Heidingsfelder

Quilted by
Mrs. Jonas Raber

Karen Witt, Minnie Prater, Mabel Fields
Winchester, Kentucky

Double Wedding Ring

Karen Witt says about this award-winning quilt, "The quilt is the traditional Double Wedding Ring pattern, but through the color scheme a secondary pattern develops. I have read all the books I can find on color and fabric selection and firmly believe that these are the most important aspects of a quilt. If the color and design are right, then a person will come closer to look at the workmanship. If

first place

1986 AQS Show & Contest Group Quilt

the color and design are poor and the workmanship outstanding, it still is not going to be a beautiful quilt. Workmanship is also very important and that is one of the main reasons this quilt has so much quilting on it.

I particularly admire the theories and ideas of Jinny Beyer. Her quilts are artistic but still look appropriate for a bed. That, to me, is the look I want to achieve – contemporary in fabric, color and design but traditional also – a compromise between the two."

Karen holds a B.S. in home

economics from Eastern Kentucky University and an M.S. in management and consumer economics from the University of Tennessee at Knoxville. She began teaching quilting classes while a County Extension Agent for Home Economics. Since leaving this position, she has been teaching classes on her own. Her work has won awards and she and Minnie have been commissioned to create a quilt to hang in the Old State Capital in Frankfort, Kentucky.

Speaking of DOUBLE WEDDING RING, Karen says, "After lots of small projects over the

years, I knew I was ready for and anxious to make a full-size quilt. But I doubted my ability to make that time commitment to the project. So, I decided to do the part I like to do best and recruit help for the parts I didn't think I could handle. I love to design and select fabrics so I did all that. I like to hand piece so I selected a pattern appropriate for that.

My friend Minnie Prater helped me piece the quilt. We logged our time – I put in over 165 hours and she contributed 95 hours to construct the top in ten months. I then developed the quilting design and hired Mabel Fields to quilt it. I ended up with a quilt that I love that was finished in a reasonable amount of time. This encouraged me to start a quilt that I am now working on all by myself – it will take me about four years to finish but I know that I can do it because of the DOUBLE WEDDING RING quilt."

Asked if she feels any differently about the quilt now, Karen replies, "YES! When I first made the quilt I couldn't stand the thought of anything happening to it so when I used it I always took it off the bed before we slept – in fact, the quilt spent a lot more

Karen Witt advises: "Continue quilting. It's a joy now and an heirloom for future generations. It's cheaper than a psychiatrist – it's a great outlet for stress. A couple of quiet hours (or even a couple of minutes) of quilting and the world looks more manageable.

DOUBLE
WEDDING
RING
102" x 88"
1986
Karen Witt
Minnie Prater
Mabel Fields

time in the closet than on the bed! Now I want to use it! It has become a real joy to me to walk into the room and see the quilt on the bed. I hope my children will appreciate it and care for it but I know it means more to me than it ever will anyone else."

About competitions, Karen says, "When I first started quilting and using fabrics, color and design differently from others around me, I was a little unsure of what I was doing. I asked myself, 'Am I on the right track?' I began entering contests. In fact, I entered my first local contest in my maiden name – in case my creation was so bad and received so many critical comments, I wouldn't be associated with it! Entering contests and winning them was a real boost to my ego! It is a wonderful feeling to win a contest such as the AQS show and have a professional judge appreciate your work. It definitely encouraged me to continue with my quilting and strive to improve."

Jody Hicks
Lexington, Kentucky

Tribute To Unknown Quilters

Jody Hicks explains, "The center block, an early Crown of Thorns, surrounded by Album (Friendship) blocks and Indian Hatchet blocks, were all found in estate sales in Missouri and are approximately 80-100 years old. I feel that this particular combination of blocks is symbolic of the lives of the women who made them. The corner blocks are North Carolina Lily, a trib-

second place

1986 AQS Show & Contest Group Quilt

ute to my own home state." Jody continues, "After machine piecing the top, I quilted it by hand very heavily, in the manner it would have been done had it been made in the time of the antique blocks."

Of her background, Jody says, "After years of making my own clothes and dabbling in most other forms of needlework, I 'tried' quilting in 1983 and have been addicted ever since. When my first completed quilt won Best of Show at the state fair, I decided to get more serious

about quilting! The Green Country Quilters Guild in Tulsa, Oklahoma, was a tremendous source of education and inspiration during my early years. Before long, I found myself teaching others and making commissioned quilts for offices. I was thrilled to have had quilts accepted in each of the first five AQS shows. Recently I have gone to Tegucigalpa, Honduras, to teach basic techniques of quilting and start a cottage industry as a mission project. I am currently designing traditional American-style quilts for them to make for sale in this country."

About her award-winning quilt, Jody explains, "This quilt started out to be just a little country-style wallhang-

ing, but as I worked with those old blocks, wondering about their makers, and as I poured more and more of myself into it, it seemed to take on a life of its own. Now that it has won two national awards and the idea has been taken up by others, it has become a symbol of our quilting heritage."

Of her show experience, Jody says, "The success of this quilt has inspired me to keep growing and reaching and learning. It gave me credibility as a teacher, which in turn has led to further expansion of my skills in techniques and design."

Jody continually reminds her students and friends: "When you go to shows don't be intimidated, be inspired!" She adds, "Except for serious artists (or those who aspire to be), I encourage others not to make something specifically for a particular competition, but to make whatever they want and find a competition to fit the quilt. Then they are spending their time on something they love, but the knowledge that it will be in a show someday keeps them doing their very best work."

"TRIBUTE TO UNKNOWN QUILTERS has become my personal statement for the preservation of the bits and pieces of quilts that are found in flea markets and estate sales. Don't just store them or make something trivial with them; do something worthwhile."

TRIBUTE TO
UNKNOWN
QUILTERS
84" x 84"
1985
Jody Hicks
and unknown
quilters

Lincoln Sampler

Ruth Dawson writes about her group and their quilting experience, "It hardly seems possible that close to six years have passed since strangers, joined by an interest in quilting, attended one of the early meetings of the newly formed Springfield, Illinois, area quilt guild and decided to get together a couple of times each month to sew. The little group con-

third place

*1986 AQS Show & Contest
Group Quilt*

sisted primarily of beginners who – with one exception – had no experience with pattern drafting and almost no knowledge of quilt construction."

Ruth continues, "Within months we decided to make a full-size quilt as a charitable project. A sampler that depicted Abraham Lincoln's life was selected from a picture in a magazine because we liked the idea of a quilt made by Springfield women that represented our community's famous resident. A complicated project, it consisted of Steps to the White House, Barrister, Little Giant, Fort Sumter, Springfield, Rail Fence and Log Cabin blocks. A major quilting pattern throughout the Lincoln Sampler is the Whig Rose design. Together, we planned, made templates, selected fabrics and with the enthusiasm that is often found in the inexperienced, we constructed totally by hand a wonderfully color-

ful and (as we later learned) well executed project that amazed us. All in all, it was a successful effort."

"Showing the quilt at AQS," Ruth explains, "was not part of our original plan. In fact, it was not considered until the quilt was completed. We entered what was probably a 'first quilt' for most of us out of our desire to raise money for charity because restrictions in Illinois law prevented us from holding a raffle. As beginners we were surprised and honored by the award. We all felt that it was a wonderfully successful example of working together and accomplishing a goal that most of us could not have achieved individually. We gained a great deal of confidence in our individual abili-

"A few members have entered competitions and received recognition but, in general, the most important aspect of our work remains the personal satisfaction received from doing the best work we can. Working with friends makes the experience far more interesting and lots more fun."

LINCOLN
SAMPLER
90" x 90"
1985
Quilt Fans
Group

ties and have gone on to execute and complete many large and/or complex projects."

Speaking further of her group, Ruth adds, "The individuals in the group remain dedicated to hand piecing and applique, usually using traditional patterns and always learning from each other's skill and experience."

Sylvia Whitesides
Lafayette, Indiana

Sunrise On The Lake

To create this award-winning quilt, Sylvia Whitesides "used the traditional Young Man's Fancy block, manipulating the blocks and using hand-dyed cottons to give an original design." All of the fabric incorporated was cotton muslin which she had "hand-dyed in shade gradations of blue through red." The quilt was machine pieced and hand quilted.

first place

*1986 AQS Show & Contest
Wall Quilt, Amateur*

Speaking of SUNRISE ON THE LAKE, Sylvia says, "This quilt was the second quilt I had ever made and my first experience in hand dyeing. What a challenge! I feel that by pushing my skills in quilt-making towards a goal such as a competition (this quilt was originally made for the 1985 Indianapolis Star Contest), I really learn and grow." Continuing, she adds, looking at the quilt now, "Because I was a novice at hand dyeing, I did not use good lightfast dyes. So now I have to be very careful about displaying

it or it fades. I also know my competence in piecing is now much better."

About her background, Sylvia says, "I have been sewing since I was a small girl, but had not made quilts until six years ago. My background is in art and interior design. My husband is a family physician and we have three young daughters, age 16 months, four, and seven. We have lived in Lafayette for three years and I love it here as there is a great quilt guild and quilting group I'm very active in."

Asked about her AQS award experience, Sylvia comments: "My husband was jealous of my quilting because I spent so much time at it; and he thought of it as another hobby that I'd leave half finished. Winning this award changed the way he viewed my quilting. It somehow made it legitimate for me to spend so much time at it. It also gave me the confidence to pursue my quilting and enter other competitions. I have since had quilts win at other shows and be published in books and magazines, which is exciting."

Talking to other quiltmakers, Sylvia says: "Even though I'm a mother with three young children, my quilting is very important to me. If I don't find time for my quilting, then little by little I have trouble coping with the kids. My husband is now very supportive of my quilting, which is great."

Sylvia continues, "My 'playroom.' is where I sew, and my kids play. This setup works great for us. The children always want to be where I am so by bringing the toys into my sewing room they can play right there and I get to sew. They have grown up with this set-up and really enjoy having me right there. There are lots of interruptions but I still get a lot more done. This room is always a mess and it's one area the kids don't have to keep so clean. I am an unorganized creative person who works well with lots of clutter!"

"I learn and grow a lot from entering competitions because I am challenging myself to do better, innovative work. Rejection is difficult but you have to understand that quilts are very subjective – keep on trying. When you do get accepted and possibly even win an award it is very exciting and fulfilling."

SUNRISE ON
THE LAKE
60" x 60"
1985
Sylvia
Whitesides

Teresa Tucker Young
Georgetown, Kentucky

1926 Collection

Teresa Tucker Young says that the pattern for 1926 COLLECTION "was based on patterns for clothing of 1926," which were then "set in a geometrical design inspired by Art Deco."

The materials incorporated in the quilt were cotton and were combined with a polyester batting. Traditional applique and piecing methods were used, and the quilt

second place

1986 AQS Show & Contest
Wall Quilt, Amateur

was hand quilted.

Teresa says of her background, "I am a native Kentuckian. I was educated at the University of Kentucky and University of Louisville. I have always been involved in art and have been making art quilts since 1985. My work is pictorial and is often social/political in nature. I am 39 years old, am married, and have two children."

Asked about her current feelings about 1926 COLLECTION, Teresa comments, "All my quilts are special to me in different ways, and I have a fondness for this one, but it's not my favorite. My recent work is a bit more serious in content and, in my judgment, better from a creative perspective."

In response to a question about the effect of the AQS award, Teresa explains, "The AQS competition was a very important confidence-builder. 1926 COLLECTION was only my second quilt, and the 1986 show was my first major show."

To other quiltmakers, Teresa says that in order to complete quilts, you "have to set priorities." She adds that she finds "having a competition deadline helps."

*"It is imperative to take the work seriously, to be disciplined –
otherwise you'll never finish anything. Because you're your own boss,
it's easy to let things get in the way of your work."*

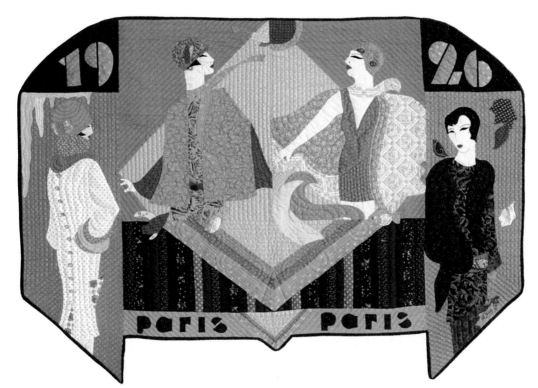

1926
COLLECTION
60" x 40"
1986
Teresa Tucker
Young

Eileen Bahring Sullivan
Columbia, South Carolina

Ribbon Of Infinity

This original-design quilt with "one continuous ribbon moving in and out of verticals (a weaving) and changing from light to dark" was Eileen Bahring Sullivan's "first experience with curved-seam piecing and a first experiment with creating a piece with two visual planes." The quilt was "machine pieced with curved two-patch units (occasionally they had to be three-patch units to complete the visual

third place

*1986 AQS Show & Contest
Wall Quilt, Amateur*

effect). The back was pieced in a manner similar to the front ground area, to continue the idea of complete unity of the quilt."

Looking back at her award-winning quilt, Eileen says, "I was quite satisfied with it from a design standpoint at the time, and it served as a 'springboard' for me in that area. Technically I feel I could have improved some areas. It was followed by several more complex pieces further exploring the ribbon theme."

A native of Connecticut, Eileen has lived in South Car-

olina for three and a half years. She holds a degree in art education, but is basically a self-taught quilter who started in 1979 with traditional work and began experimenting with design in 1983. She adds, "Now all my time goes into quiltmaking and I continue to compete annually, occasionally lecturing and judging."

Eileen says winning the AQS award had "A TREMENDOUS effect! It was early in my career of competition and gave me a tremendous boost in confidence. Recognition by 'the quilting world' also brought about great changes in my family's attitude toward my work which, until then,

Photo: Renee Ittner-McManus/*The State*, Columbia, SC.

had not been taken seriously. It also brought about my first trip to Paducah which opened up a whole new aspect of the quilt world to me. I returned home determined to continue exploring design possibilities and haven't stopped yet!"

To other quiltmakers, Eileen says: "Strive for growth with each new piece (smaller pieces help) and these skills will begin to be incorporated unconsciously in future pieces. Competition is not for everyone, but all quiltmakers should 'share their work' with other quilters at local shows and events. For those interested in competing, be honest with yourself in evaluating your work. Become familiar with the standards required for a piece to stand up against others, and don't settle for less when you're making it. Even if the judges don't agree with you, you'll be satisfied that the piece is the best it could be, and realize that judging is still quite subjective. What wins in one show might fare quite differently elsewhere. Learn from written critiques, but don't let one disappointing experience keep you from continuing. Choose shows that are 'right' for the type of work you are entering."

"Capitalize on your strengths – artistic or technical – and be conscious of areas of work that need improvement. Challenge yourself with each new piece to gain control over at least one more element."

RIBBON OF
INFINITY
58" x 58"
1985
Eileen Bahring
Sullivan

Jane Blair
Conshohocken, Pennsylvania

Night Bloom

Jane Blair says, "My work begins with the quilt blocks created and named by quilters of the past. From these beginnings, with colors, fabric and design, I find it a challenge to create a new approach to something as old as a traditional quilt block."

Jane is a professional quilt artist and teacher, living in Conshohocken, Pennsylvania, who specializes in new

first place

*1986 AQS Show & Contest
Wall Quilt, Professional*

design possibilities from traditional pattern beginnings. Though graduated with a B.S. in education from West Chester University, she is self taught in quiltmaking and has devoted a regular eight hour day to it for more than nineteen years. She has taught quiltmaking and quilt design regularly in the Philadelphia area since 1976, and has taught and also lectured in many other states. Her quilts are often seen in magazines and invitational group and solo exhibits throughout the country. She

is a frequent contributor to quilting magazines and has had her quilts on five *Quilter's Newsletter Magazine* covers.

NIGHT BLOOM is composed of Basket of Scraps blocks in rows of alternating direction, with applique stems added. Jane explains, "Each block is colored individually. Shapes are dropped out of some blocks to create blooming vine on a wall." The quilt is hand-pieced, appliqued, and quilted. Asked if she feels differently about the quilt now than she did at the time she made it,

she replies, "No! I did what I wanted at that time. The quilts made since then have satisfied the same creative need." What she would most like people to notice about the quilt is "How much color can do for the ordinary!" And she adds she would also like people to realize, "It's only one of many I've made."

With regard to her AQS award she says, "Because success is measured by money earned, every money award raises one's self-esteem and the level of respect from others to some degree. It has not or could not change what I

"I am interested in innovative design and color, but still want the end result to be more pleasing to the eye than shocking to the soul; somewhere between the faded gems of the past and the vivid harshness of the present. If my work looks traditional to some and contemporary to others, I have achieved the blending of old and new which is my goal."

NIGHT BLOOM
56" x 72"
1986
Jane Blair

am doing – making quilts."

To other quiltmakers she says, "Do your very best. Don't copy others. Produce and produce more! Don't let someone else's opinion (including a judge's) rule what you do or how you do it."

Arlene Lane
Leona Valley, California

An Old English Flower Garden

The technique Arlene Lane used to create AN OLD ENGLISH FLOWER GARDEN is *broderie perse*, the appliqueing of figures cut from a floral fabric. The quilt was put together with all-cotton muslin and a split cotton batting, and was heavily quilted, with all major quilting designs trapuntoed. The center rose and flowers were trapuntoed against a closely stippled center background.

About the quilt, Arlene says, "It has won numerous awards, including the award

second place

*1986 AQS Show & Contest
Wall Quilt, Professional*

for merit for technical expertise at the San Diego Visions quilt show 1987. It is the feature cover quilt on *Quilts Galore,* by Diana McClun & Laura Nownes."

Of her background Arlene says, "I have taught quilting since 1978, primarily in the Southern California area, but have traveled and taught in a number of other states as well. In 1984 I authored and published a book on hand applique – *Applique, An Effective New Approach.* I have taken a break from teaching to help my daughter-in-law with the arrival of triplets. I

have been working on a new *broderie perse* quilt that is quite different from this first one."

Asked to comment on the effect of her AQS show experience, Arlene says, "It made me realize how important it is for quiltmakers to share their work with others. I believe all work done from the heart serves to inspire others. It has inspired me to learn more and do more."

To other quiltmakers she says: "Deep down, way down in each of us is that special quilt, an heirloom struggling to surface, to come out and express our most creative self. Work to please yourself and you will marvel at what can happen."

*Living in an era when quilts can be made in a weekend and supplies
and equipment to serve that purpose are so readily available,
we sometimes long to savor the pleasure of a uniquely designed quilt top –
to enjoy the satisfaction of the quilting stitches as a well-thought-out
and planned design emerges, giving a new dimension to our piece.*

AN OLD
ENGLISH
FLOWER
GARDEN
41" x 49"
1986
Arlene Lane

Marion L. Huyck
Evanston, Illinois

Nothing Gold Can Stay

Marion explains that the center of NOTHING GOLD CAN STAY "is an original pieced design, stylized to look like a dandelion in all of its various stages. The appliqued borders, more representative dandelions, are adapted from Art Nouveau." She continues, "The fabrics in the quilt are all cotton, some hand-dyed. The center of the quilt is hand and machine-

third place

1986 AQS Show & Contest Wall Quilt, Professional

pieced. The left, right and bottom borders are hand-appliqued and reverse appliqued. The entire quilt is hand-quilted."

Of her background, Marion says, "Full-time quiltmaking occupied a significant 12 years of my adult life, from 1978 - 1989, while I raised my three sons. Both before

and since, I have been and am again a full-time high school English teacher. My quilting is now my 'summer career.'"

Talking about the development of her quilt, Marion says, "I have always been interested in the cycles of nature, the way living things change in shape and color, the way living things have different forms at birth, maturity, and senescence. The dandelion is a particularly good example. It has the added wonder of sharp, jagged leaves contrasted with its soft button flower. Best of all, it's 'white hair' drifts away to plant itself later and

begin a new cycle. Personally the dandelion is a family symbol. I have always hailed a field of yellow as one of the first joyous bursts of spring. My sons used to bring me handfuls as gifts."

Looking at NOTHING GOLD CAN STAY now, Marion says, "Many of my quilts were 'over' for me once I had finished them because the challenge came in making them, and that process ended. A few quilts, surprisingly to me, were different. They took on a new life for me when I saw them whole and hung. They were more than I expected. I saw new things in them, and their symbolism had a power and effect that went beyond my planning and expectation. NOTHING GOLD CAN STAY is like that for me now."

Her advice to other quiltmakers: "To borrow a phrase... 'do what you love. The rewards will follow.'"

"Most of the awards I have won have surprised me, particularly the AQS award. The first award is always internal, the joy of seeing an idea come to life and become 'fact.' The public awards are an affirmation and an encouragement to continue doing what I loved in the first place."

NOTHING
GOLD
CAN STAY
71" x 57"
©1985
Marion L.
Huyck

Museum of AQS
Collection

Quilt Show & Contest

1987

The third American Quilter's Society Quilt Show & Contest was held April 24-28, 1987, at the Executive Inn Riverfront in Paducah, Kentucky.

Judges for quilt awards were Virginia Avery, Port Chester, NY; Jean Johnson, Maplewood, NJ; Helen Thompson, Lexington, KY. Categories and category award sponsors were as follows:

Best of Show, American Quilter's Society
Gingher Award for Workmanship, Gingher, Inc.
First Quilt Award, American Quilter's Society
Traditional Pieced, Amateur, Hobbs Bonded Fibers
Traditional Pieced, Professional, Coats & Clark
Innovative Pieced, Amateur, Fairfield Processing Corp.
Innovative Pieced, Professional, Gutcheon Patchworks

Applique, Amateur, V.I.P
Applique, Professional, Mountain Mist
Other Techniques, Amateur, Extra Special Products, Inc.
Other Techniques, Professional, Viking White
Theme: Log Cabin, Amateur/Professional, That Patchwork Place
Group/Team, Amateur/Professional, Swiss-Metrosene, Inc.
Wall Quilt, Amateur, Yours Truly/Burdett Publications
Wall Quilt, Professional, Fiskars

In each category three awards were made: 1st place, $700; 2nd place, $500; 3rd place, $300. The Gingher Award for Excellence of Workmanship was a $1,000 award; the AQS Best of Show Award, $10,000; and the First Quilt Award, $200.

The exhibit included quilts representing 50 states, and Canada, Japan and Switzerland. During the show, many of the people who attended voted for their favorite quilt, and a Viewer's Choice award was later made.

A quilted fashion contest sponsored by Hobbs Bonded Fibers was a popular new attraction at the 1987 show, and a multitude of quilt-related activities in the Paducah area were sponsored by other organizations and businesses throughout the weekend.

Sharon Rauba
Woodridge, Illinois

Autumn Radiance

To develop this quilt, Sharon Rauba collected leaves on autumn walks. She explains, "I wanted to make a different type of leaf quilt. A Trip-Around-the-World setting of small leaves of different shapes and colors seemed like a good idea. I planned each border from the middle out using what fabric I had at home. Each additional border added a

best of show

1987 AQS Show & Contest

new look to the whole design."

Sharon says she has enjoyed knitting, embroidering and sewing clothes since she was a child, and in 1980 "became interested in quilting and read everything in the library on the subject, trying out all the different techniques." She adds, "Quilting has added beauty, growth, and friendship to my life."

Speaking of this winning quilt she says, "I tried to express my love of nature. This quilt also marks the

time when I took all that I had learned in my first 3-4 years of quilting and made it my own. Studying techniques and designs and practicing on my first projects brought me to the point of wanting to go on my own, to design my quilt, to do my best work and to make the quilt that only I could make."

She continues, "This quilt was my very best effort – just the amount of work and dedication needed to finish it is staggering when I look back on it. I will always love AUTUMN RADIANCE because

it came from my heart. In the years since 1983 when it was started, I have grown and changed, and so have my quilts and the way I approach my work. But AUTUMN RADIANCE marks the time when I first put myself into my work and made what pleased me."

To other quiltmakers Sharon says, "Learn everything you can from all the wonderful teachers and information available. Then at some point step off onto your own path and make the quilts that only you can make. Ask for advice and learn from others but in the end make your own choices so your quilt will be a reflection of the maker. Welcome mistakes, shortages of fabric, design problems, etc. Dealing with them will force you to grow and stretch. Correcting mistakes and putting in the amount of time and effort necessary to produce the desired result are worth it in the end. I am trying to work in an increasingly open way – to let the quilt just happen – and I find it an absorbing and fun experience."

"Winning was a wonderful thrill, but also very scary. All of a sudden, my work was publicly scrutinized, judged, commented on, praised, and yes, criticized. Since my work is personal, I felt naked, exposed and uncomfortable in many ways. When I came to realize that my quilt was my best work done to please myself and winning was secondary, I felt better. That lesson has strengthened me."

AUTUMN
RADIANCE
81" x 93"
1986
Sharon Rauba

Museum of AQS Collection

Beverly Mannisto Williams
Cadillac, Michigan

Victorian Fantasy Of Feathers And Lace

Beverly Mannisto Williams says, "I gravitate toward medallion oval shapes and love feathered plumes and hand stitching." Three-fourths of the quilting motifs in this whole-cloth quilt are Beverly's original designs and a few are from books. Beverly explains, "The border designed by Marge Murphy instigated this project. I adapted a Swedish design in the center and used a Finnish bobbin lace edging

gingher award

for workmanship
1987 AQS Show & Contest

in memory of parents and grandparents."

To create VICTORIAN FANTASY OF FEATHERS AND LACE, Beverly pinned 90" wide 100% cotton unbleached muslin fabric to the pattern she had developed and traced lightly with a No. 2-1/2 pencil. Light brown thread was used for the quilted designs and off-white on the grid work.

Of her background, Beverly says, "I have always craved to create crafts and sewing projects. When my sons were young I stayed home and did seamstress work for many years. When I

came upon quilting and bobbin lace I found comfort and satisfaction in making long-term projects. I hope to be faithful to these crafts as long as I am capable. Although I have had some quilt and bobbin lace lessons I have no formal art training but hope that is to my advantage. I have taught some quilting and bobbin lace and hope to get more involved in the future. I am content at this time to pursue the quilting and lacemaking, work part time in a fabric department, and teach a niece and granddaughter the joys of sewing."

Beverly adds, "When a person such as myself who has no art training can produce an idea, everyone must possess creative abilities. My quilting

tends to move very slowly, but if dedicated anyone can finish a major project. I am also a bobbin lacemaker and I felt a real obligation and mission to create a piece of work on which to showcase handmade lace. Every stitch in the quilt and twist of the thread in the lace is worked (and occasionally reworked) by hand. I hope my first-time competition quilt will be an inspiration to fellow quilters."

Speaking of her quilt, Beverly comments, "I feel about this quilt as I do my children. They are yours for a time to mold and shape. Although you will miss them, there comes a time to share them with others as they grow and leave home to begin new lives." Beverly says winning the AQS award was "a real confidence builder!" She explains, "All of my years of home sewing and crafting seem to have led up to the privilege of being honored with receiving quilt awards." In 1987 this quilt was designated a masterpiece quilt by the Masters Guild of the National Quilting Association.

To other quiltmakers, Beverly suggests, "Sample many techniques (possibly your own) on small projects until you find the ones you would enjoy enough to work on a

"I had never been a competitive person until I met up with quilting and realized this was something I loved enough to participate in.
The awards have shown my family and friends that I take this more seriously than a hobby. Quilting and lacemaking have become a way of life for me. I've found 'what I wanted to do when I grow up.'"

VICTORIAN
FANTASY
OF FEATHERS
AND LACE
89" x 100"
1986
Beverly Mannisto
Williams

larger scale. Respect and follow your own instincts, working to satisfy yourself. Take lessons in techniques you are not confident in. Be selective in all aspects, from designing to techniques, focusing time and energy on one worthwhile project. There is nothing as rewarding to oneself as the pride, peace of mind and self-worth one can find in a creative effort. Desire, dedication, discipline, practice, patience, perseverance are the key ingredients."

Judy A. Fitzgerald
Lincoln, Nebraska

Mariner's Compass With Feathered Squares

Judy Fitzgerald began quilting in 1971 when her husband was in graduate school. She explains, "I checked all the books on quilting out of the public library: a grand total of one. The pattern I selected was Dolly Madison's Star. (How was I to know it was not a beginner pattern?) The only quilts I had ever seen were in books. My first quilting stitches were about 1/2 inch

first place

*1987 AQS Show & Contest
Traditional Pieced, Ama*

long. But having committed myself...I persevered. By the time I finished I not only knew how to quilt, but I was addicted."

Her totally hand-sewn MARINER'S COMPASS WITH FEATHERED SQUARES was inspired by a photo of an antique quilt in Myron and Patsy Orlofsky's *Quilts in America*. (She added the Mariner's Compass.)

Judy comments, "I call this quilt my trauma quilt. Working in a hoop, I had part of one border left to do when my (then) small daughter brought me a freshly painted

black acrylic picture and dropped it on the quilt. I scooped the quilt up, rushed to the kitchen sink and plunged the stained area into cold water. All of the paint except one tiny ring came out, but the gold fabric which had been so carefully pretested for colorfastness bled onto the back in big pools. I decided to finish the quilt anyway and live with the discoloration."

She continues, "Just as I was finishing up, a needle slipped and buried itself at both ends in the border. Getting the needle out caused a small hole to appear. I rewove this by using threads pulled from remnants of the

PHOTO: BARRY'S OF LINCOLN, NE

border fabric. I then was faced with washing the quilt to remove traces of blue fabric marker, but I was afraid of more fading. I thought the best solution was to keep the quilt flat. My husband washed the driveway down with a good grease remover. We laid the quilt out and used the hose to run gallons of water through the quilt. It worked! Only one small discolored area remained."

Judy adds, "Making the quilt gave me credibility in my own eyes as a quilter. Just the fact that it was selected for AQS competition was tremendously gratifying and the whole Paducah experience is one of the high points of my life. But winning awards has had positive and negative effects. On the positive side I (and perhaps those close to me) see myself as a more well rounded person, as having achieved something outside of home and community. More important, though, is that this quilt will not be forgotten. It is so well documented because of its stellar career that it will be remembered and my name recalled long after I and all who knew me are gone. On the negative side it is somewhat intimidat-

*"I don't make quilts for contests. I make quilts because I have to.
If you can't say things one way, you learn to say them another – you give a
bouquet of flowers or write a song. Quilts are my language. I speak
through them and they certainly "speak" to me. They are like my diary."*

MARINER'S
COMPASS
WITH
FEATHERED
SQUARES
90" x 105"
1986
Judy A.
Fitzgerald

ing to do such a celebrated piece of work. Everything you do thereafter is judged by the standard of THE QUILT."

Asked to give advice, Judy says, "I like to see quilts that are intensely personal and tell me something about the maker. 'Plastic' quilts that are so perfect that they are devoid of all personality don't speak to me."

Leigh Pollpeter
West Bend, Wisconsin

The Boston Commons Quilt

Leigh Pollpeter says her quilt is based on the *Boston Commons Quilt* by Helen and Blanche Young. She explains, "After taking a class with Blanche Young on Trip Around the World quilts, I was inspired with their techniques and then made my THE BOSTON COMMONS QUILT."

All cotton fabrics were used. The quilt was con-

second place

1987 AQS Show & Contest Traditional Pieced, Ama

structed using the multiple template, as directed in Helen and Blanche Young's book. Blue washout marker was used for marking the quilting and the piece was quilted in a

Hinterberg frame.

About her background, Leigh says, "I have been quilting for 10 years. I have three children, Steven, Andrew and Sarah, and a very patient and helpful husband, Todd."

Leigh would most like

people to know: "The quilt was made for my mother and father-in-law, Betty and Ronald Pollpeter. All that they specified was that it was to have the color green in it. They didn't care what colors I chose with it or what design I picked out. I love traditional patchwork and chose the *Boston Commons Quilt*."

Asked if she feels any differently about the quilt now, Leigh says, "I love the beauty of the hand quilting and the intricate designs. I no longer have time to hand quilt and it is very precious to me."

Speaking about her AQS show experience, specifically the award, Leigh comments, "It gave me the confidence that I needed for me to start my own business making miniature quilts."

"Know in your heart that you did the best job you possibly could, and do not get discouraged, because in the quilting competition, today, you're competing with artists."

THE BOSTON
COMMONS
QUILT
89" x 104"
1986
Leigh Pollpeter

Jeanne Tanamachi
St. Paul, Minnesota

Six Pointed Stars

"I enjoyed making this quilt so much that it would have a special place in my heart even without the honors it has received," says Jeanne Tanamachi about SIX POINTED STARS.

The pattern used is the traditional six-pointed star. About the inspiration, Jeanne says, "The idea for piecing the stars in a kaleidoscopic

third place

1987 AQS Show & Contest Traditional Pieced, Ama

fashion came from a class I took with Jinny Beyer, who demonstrated what could be done with an eight-pointed star."

Jeanne used 100% cottons for the quilt, with many Hoffman Woodblocks. The top is hand-pieced and quilted. She adds, "Quilting lines were marked in two ways, some with a silver pencil and some

with needle-tracking, because I did not want my marks to show."

Of her background, Jeanne says, "I was born in 1949 in Winona, Minnesota, and have lived in Minnesota all my life. I earned a B.A. in American history at the University of Minnesota, and did some additional course work in library science. I worked for the University of Minnesota, first as an account clerk and then as a cataloger in the library, until I decided to stay at home after the birth of my second child. I became interested in needlework in the early 1970's as a form of relaxation. When I was introduced to quilting at the Kansas Quilt Symposium in 1978, it took over my creative life. I am a member of Minnesota Quilters, and have worked on three of our annual conferences. I am also active in the Minnesota Quilt Project, studying the older

quilts of our state. I am currently employed at a quilt shop in St. Paul, Minnesota."

Asked about her current feelings for her quilt SIX POINTED STAR, she says, "It has become like an old friend to me. I made it when my children were two and six years old and life was much less organized than it is now. It reminds me that it is possible to do good work under difficult circumstances."

In regards to her award, Jeanne says, "Most importantly, it has caused me to take my own talents seriously. Other people feel that way, too; it's converted a few skeptics among my family and friends. Opportunities for growth came my way after winning the AQS award. It gave me the confidence to keep on trying and growing. I feel that my workmanship, while it is not perfect, is not an obstacle to trying out new ideas."

"The quilt you make should please you most of all. You will not win every competition you enter. That does not make you less of a person, nor does it mean your quilt was bad. You are the first and last judge of that quilt."

SIX POINTED
STARS
85" x 96"
1986
Jeanne
Tanamachi

Martha B. Skelton
Vicksburg, Mississippi

New York Beauty

"This is a very old design with many variations," says Martha B. Skelton about NEW YORK BEAUTY. She continues, "In this quilt design, I set the blocks on the diagonal with pieced sashing and stars at the intersections. I chose to make it oblong so that the design might be more complete."

She adds, "The fabrics are 100% cotton, the batting

first place

1987 AQS Show & Contest
Traditional Pieced, Pro

polyester. It is mostly hand-pieced, with the long seams machine stitched. The feather quilting follows the circular shapes and the remainder is quilted by the piece."

Of her background Martha says, "I was born in West Virginia, grew up in Oklahoma, graduated from the University of Oklahoma, and have lived in Mississippi since 1947. I started quilting at age 15. I started teaching quilting in 1971, am a demonstrating member of the Mississippi Craftsmen's

Guild, a participant at Smithsonian Festival of American Folklife in Washington, D.C., and have coordinated the State Fair Quilting Bee for many years. I attend shows and symposiums, taking classes and reading to broaden my knowledge. I have had work published in books and magazines and have quilts in the permanent collections of Mountain Mist, the Mississippi State Histori-

cal Museum and the American Quilter's Society."

About NEW YORK BEAUTY, Martha would like people to know that "while it follows a very old pattern, it is unique in that there is no other quilt exactly like this one." She explains, "I drafted my pattern to include various parts of old examples I studied; no one other quilt contains all the components." She adds that her feelings about the quilt have not changed. She says, "I still like it."

Of her show experience Martha says, "Making this quilt satisfied a compelling need to make the design after studying many examples, both in hand and in books. It pushed me to draft the pattern in the way I envisioned it should be rather than compromise by using an available one. Having it win an award was wonderful and then to become a part of the AQS Collection and then the further recognition of being asked to teach. That was quite an accolade for a teacher."

To other quiltmakers, Martha says: "Make a quilt because you want to. If you are thinking about entering it

"Quilting has brought me many friends and much joy, carried me through grief and loss, and inspired me to keep reaching for new goals and to always be willing to share this interest with others."

NEW YORK
BEAUTY
77" x 90"
1986
Martha B.
Skelton

Museum of AQS Collection

in a competition, comply with the rules. Be ready for acceptance or rejection, praise or criticism. Implementing the impersonal critique helps you grow in skill. Enjoy your work. Satisfy yourself and if others like it, that is good. Some folks thrive on competition, others are very uncomfortable competing. Finally, please yourself and especially enjoy your work."

Jane R. Long
Cary, North Carolina

Bountiful Stars

Jane R. Long started quilting in 1981 – becoming the first quilter in her family. BOUNTIFUL STARS was the fifth large piece made by this self-taught quilter, who completed three large pieces before attending even her first quilt lecture.

Discussing the quilt, Jane says, "The piecework pattern for BOUNTIFUL STARS is an original design with strong

second place

1987 AQS Show & Contest Traditional Pieced, Pro

traditional influences. A love for the quilting stitch is exhibited in BOUNTIFUL STARS, with cable and feathered designs leaning toward an Amish influence. The quilt top was constructed, layered with batting and backing, and quilted on a large scroll-style frame. The project was totally hand-pieced and quilted, with quilting no farther apart than ⅜".

She continues, "All of my quilts have given me great personal satisfaction. Each quilt represents a new challenge to me as a quiltmaker.

Having work recognized on a national level in shows such as the AQS show reinforces my feelings of accomplishment as a quiltmaker and helps to stimulate me toward new accomplishments in my work." Jane tells us she enjoys teaching quilting and spreading her enthusiasm for the craft.

Of this particular quilt Jane says "It was probably the most time-consuming of all the quilts I have made to date. Competitively, it has also been the most successful...I still hold it in highest regard."

To other quiltmakers making quilts and entering them in competitions, she says: "So many elements of creativity can be addressed in the evaluation of a quilt. Design, color, craftsmanship, as well as the sense of accomplishment in having completed a work, original to the maker, are all elements of quilting. Each competition is a new experience, and the outcome of competition can never be second guessed. The results can, however, be a good tool by which to measure and compare one's work in relation to that of one's peers. The potential for growth and self-expression in quilting is endless, and feeling oneself grow can be the greatest personal satisfaction."

"The many hours of quilting on BOUNTIFUL STARS helped me work through the death of my father, a very emotional time in my life. The accomplishments of this quilt, I dedicate to his memory."

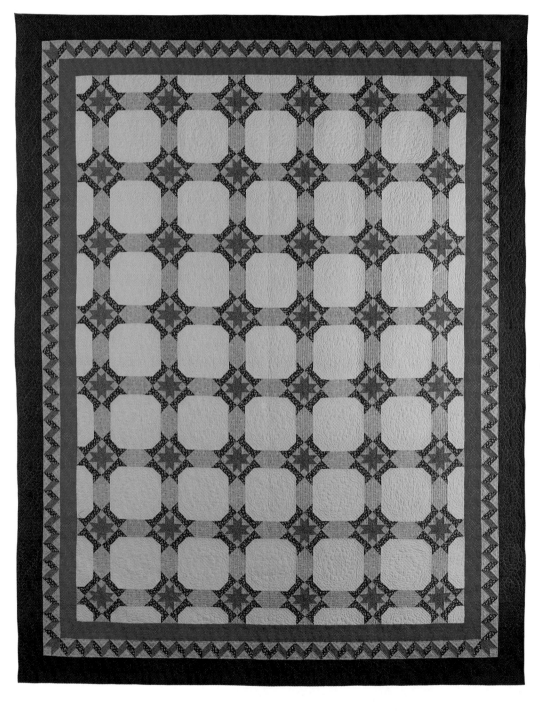

BOUNTIFUL
STARS
90" x 113"
1986
Jane R. Long

Susan B. Wolff
West Redding, Connecticut

My Twelve Ring Circus

Susan B. Wolff explains, "A traditional Carpenter's Wheel block was used to create MY TWELVE RING CIRCUS. The blocks were pieced from scraps which were then repeated in the border to 'pull the quilt together.' A tan print was used as a background fabric to obtain the overall effect of a colorful rustic quilt."

All fabrics used in the

third place

1987 AQS Show & Contest Traditional Pieced, Pro

quilt are cotton, the batt is a low loft polyester batt, and the quilting thread is cotton-wrapped polyester. The piecing was done by machine; the quilting was done by hand with the quilt in a hoop.

Speaking of the quilt's design, Susan explains, "When I decide on a quilt, I always remember that not only will it go on a bed, but someone could be stuck in that bed with the flu and just bored. I like to give that person something extra to look at." In MY TWELVE RING CIRCUS, that "something extra to look at" is five extra fabrics in the pieced border. "The person must figure out which extra fabrics are not used in the pieced blocks!"

Of her background, Susan says, "I am a homemaker and mother of four grown children, and am currently taking courses in geology at Yale in addition to teaching quilting. Though I have enjoyed needlework all my life, it wasn't until the late 1970's that I began to explore quilting. I learned by reading and experimenting. Soon I began teaching and working in a quilt shop and quickly gained experience which led me to designing. I am a traditional quilter and particularly enjoy teaching beginners."

To other quiltmakers, Susan says: "Please yourself first. You can't be truly creative if you are always trying to satisfy the standards of an imaginary judge. The best competition is with yourself. Learn, improve and strive to make each quilt a little better than the last one."

"I began making this quilt as a gift for my son. Somewhere along the way, friends started urging me to enter it in the AQS competition. I felt very honored when I won the award – but in the long run my greatest satisfaction has come from seeing the pleasure and pride my son takes in his quilt."

MY TWELVE
RING
CIRCUS
84" x 105"
1987
Susan B. Wolff

Sylvia Pickell
Sumter, South Carolina

Escape From Circle City

While developing the original design for ESCAPE FROM CIRCLE CITY, Sylvia Pickell drafted several traditional patterns to fit into circle motifs. She says, "It was designed and created as therapy or a catharsis. I was very angry and frustrated over the results of the Great American Quilt Festival I in 1986. I 'threw together' this quilt in a few weeks. The blacks and

first place

1987 AQS Show & Contest Innovative Pieced, Ama

grays were because I was in a 'dark' mood. The 'escape' was my attempt to break away from traditional into contemporary." She adds, "It completely absolved all the anger and in fact evoked much humor as people commented on the tongue-in-cheek manner of poking fun at traditional quiltmaking."

To construct the quilt, Sylvia used cottons and polyblends produced for quilt and dressmaking. Some fabrics from the 1950's were also included. Sylvia adds that most fabrics used in the quilt

were "already on-hand." The quilt was machine-pieced, with a small amount of hand applique also used. All curved areas were pieced using freezer paper templates. The quilt was hand-quilted.

A professional quiltmaker since 1985, Sylvia works on consignment or for competition. She also restores and conserves quilts, appraises them, judges shows, and lectures and teaches workshops. Her work is in several corporate collections and wins many awards. Her style varies from traditional to contemporary and innovative, and she

adds, "Lately I often use hand marbled fabrics I design."

Regarding her AQS award, Sylvia says, "This award was the incentive to become a professional quiltmaker and designer. It showed that I had recognizable expertise and that I could market and develop this aspect if I wished. On the other hand – this being only my third full-size quilt – the award thrust me into competition at professional levels. I had not yet developed fully enough as a quiltmaker to compete at that level and it has proven discouraging."

"If you desire to continue your learning experience and continue growing as a quiltmaker, you should strive to have a piece for competition as often as possible, but only pieces you enjoy making or feel compelled to make from your inner self."

ESCAPE FROM
CIRCLE CITY
76" x 86"
©1986
Sylvia Pickell

Museum of AQS Collection

Jan Lanahan
Walkersville, Maryland

Reach For The Stars

About REACH FOR THE STARS, Jan Lanahan says "In this pattern of my own design, I wanted the quilt to give the viewer the feeling of flying over fields."

She explains, "I used all types of fabric – cottons, flannels, satins – everything out of my scrapbag, overdying and bleaching to get the desired effect. The quilt is hand pieced and hand quilted." She adds, "I used

second place

1987 AQS Show & Contest
Innovative Pieced, Ama

hand whipstitching on the back so that the quilt is reversible."

Speaking of her background, Jan says, "I was born

and raised in Australia and met my husband, Mike, a U.S. Air Force officer, there. After our marriage we were stationed in different areas of the United States and Europe. My educational

background is in art and dress design. The combination of both works very well in quilting. I have two daughters, Kylee-Anne and Julie-Anne. They are also interested in art careers."

Asked if she feels any differently about the quilt today, Jan replies, "No. I feel that I accomplished all that I had set out to do."

About her AQS show experience, Jan comments, "This gave me the inspiration and enthusiasm to design and create two more prize-winning AQS quilts."

To other quiltmakers, Jan says, "Try it and enjoy; I have met wonderful interesting people through my quilts. Competitions have broadened my artistic outlook."

"REACH FOR THE STARS is a tribute to the crew of the Challenger. My first instinct as a quilter was to make a quilt for each family member of the Challenger crew (quilts give hugs when you wrap them around you), but I realized that was impossible so I decided to make one special quilt as a tribute."

REACH FOR
THE STARS
66" x 82"
1986
Jan Lanahan

Museum of AQS Collection

Jane Carter
Kalamazoo, Michigan

Unraveled Memory

UNRAVELED MEMORY was Jane Carter's first quilt. She designed it in a class and adds that she thinks her teacher was "a little baffled" when she indicated what she hoped to accomplish in the design of this quilt.

"In this quilt," Jane explains, "I wanted to both piece and applique because I wasn't sure which technique I would like best. I don't know

third place

1987 AQS Show & Contest Innovative Pieced, Ama

the name of the block, but the design is rather simple. I hand drew the applique part and 'floated' the foreground on the background. I have always liked this design device of floating one thing on the top of another. Everything is done by hand using all cotton fabric and low-loft batting."

Continuing, Jane says, "Making this quilt has had a profound effect on my life.

Now I enjoy many quilting friends and have become active in the Kalamazoo Log Cabin Quilters, a group of approximately 100 very diverse, enthusiastic and supportive quilters." Jane adds, "I don't know that winning the award has affected me that much. It gave me confidence, and I'm proud of having been honored by AQS and the show's sponsors. But, now, having attended three AQS shows, I realize how many superior quilts are shown each year, and that, although the winners may be the 'best of the best,' a certain amount of simple luck was part of my winning

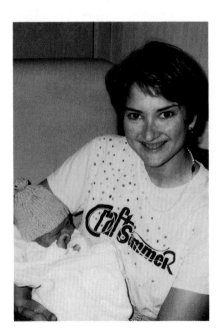

a ribbon."

Jane is a research biochemist who also enjoys artistic expression. She comments, "Quilting makes sense for me because I like sewing and fabric."

Asked to give advice for other quiltmakers, Jane says, "On making quilts, I would advise quilters who are dissatisfied with a particular fabric composition to think in terms of value alone and to add a few more fabrics with this in mind. Also, don't over plan quilts. Let the quilt help lead the process."

"On entering competitions, I would advise quilters to enter because they want to share a beautiful quilt, not to take the judges' comments too seriously, and to look at these comments as constructive criticism based on the opinion of just one or two people. Also, I hope quilt show entrants keep in mind the person for whom the quilt was made and what was learned while making the quilt."

"Now I look at this quilt and think it is very dark and lacks sparkle, definition. The dark and grayed colors were safe for me to work with at that time. Today I am more confident and like to express myself with vivid, clear colors. However, I feel very sentimental about this quilt. I could never part with it."

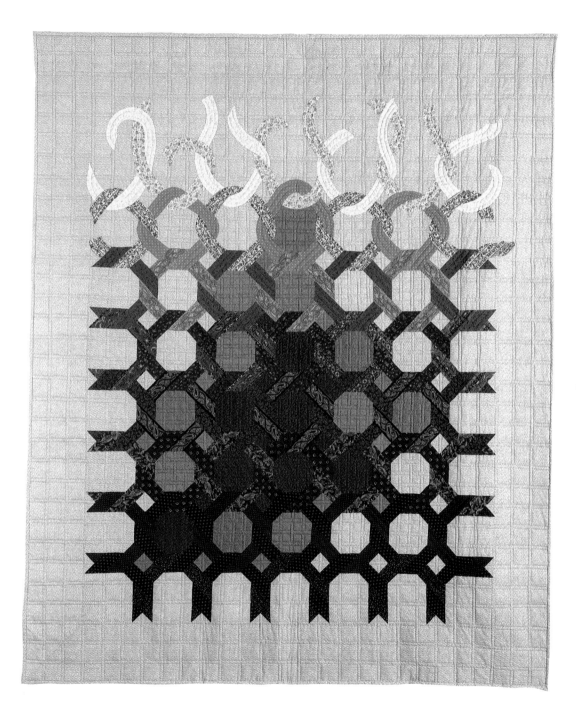

UNRAVELED
MEMORY
79" x 79"
1987
Jane Carter

Alison Goss
Hockessin, Delaware

Sundays In The Garden

Alison Goss is a self-taught quiltmaker with a varied background as a "schoolteacher, environmentalist, production sewer, and wife and mother." She has been teaching quilting classes for ten years, and now travels nationwide to give workshops and lectures. Much of her work has explored the use of strip piecing to translate themes

first place

1987 AQS Show & Contest Innovative Pieced, Pro

from nature into quilts; she concentrates on the use of color and design to create quilts which are visually exciting and challenging.

To develop SUNDAYS IN THE GARDEN, Alison says that no pattern was used. She explains, "I designed the quilt 'on the wall' in my studio, using a strip-piecing approach adapted from my bargello quilts. The design was strongly influenced by

Impressionist art, especially Monet's paintings."

She continues, "The materials are 100% cotton, with a cotton/poly batting. I made up lots of strip sets, then cut them up, using the Fibonacci series to determine the widths, and used them to create a 'picture' on my wall. I quilted by hand, in a free-form design, which was inspired by the patterns created by snow melting on a hillside."

Asked what she would like people to know about the quilt, Alison replies, "Although I started piecing this quilt in January 1986, it was pinned to my wall, about one-third finished, for months; I had to finish it very quickly in August, when we found that we were moving to Delaware in a few weeks. I was forced to work quickly and intuitively, and was surprised to find that it came out so well when I hadn't spent time pondering each design decision. It taught me to work more quickly, and

trust myself."

Alison continues, "Winning a first place award was very gratifying, and I keep the plaque on a shelf near my sewing machine, for encouragement when my work seems to be getting bogged down. It made me feel very good to find out that other people reacted in such a positive way to my work. I used plaid fabrics for the first time in this quilt, and was very excited about the color effects they create; I have been using lots of plaids since then, especially in my recent work."

To other quiltmakers, Alison says: "Your quilts should be an expression of *yourself*. It is hard to be creative if you are worried about whether other people will like your quilt, or whether you have followed all the 'rules' correctly. If you have made your quilt to satisfy yourself, then it's wonderful if it wins an award in a competition, but you'll still love it if it doesn't."

"I worried that this quilt lacked 'depth' when I first made it, because I had sewed it up so quickly. I have changed my mind since then, realizing that it expresses a lot of what I was thinking about at the time."

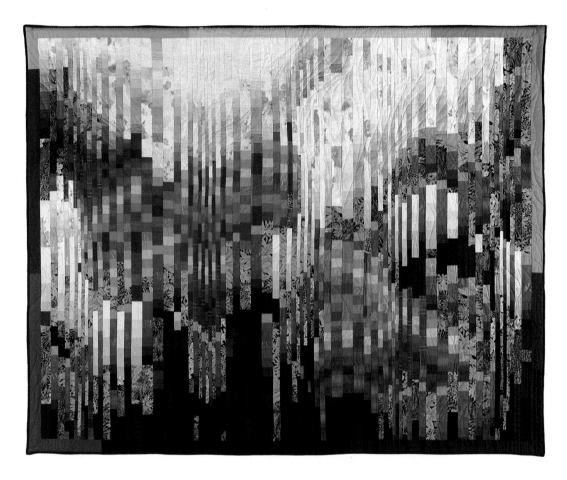

SUNDAYS
IN THE
GARDEN
84" x 68"
©1986
Alison Goss

Betty Ekern Suiter
Racine, Wisconsin

Isometric I

This original-design quilt by Betty Ekern Suiter was inspired by a 3-D workshop taught by Chris Wolf Edmonds. To execute the design, Betty used all 100% cotton fabrics, which she cut with a rotary cutter and pieced by machine. She combined this top with a cotton batting and then hand quilted the work in a hoop.

Betty says that, unlike

second place

*1987 AQS Show & Contest
Innovative Pieced, Pro*

many quilters who tend to work with only applique or only pieced quilt designs, she actually alternates between the two types of design and construction. She says she is currently making her 31st quilt, having won 150 ribbons thus far. Her quilts have been in 12 magazines and in one other book.

Though she feels her quilts are traditional in style, Betty adds that most of her designs are original. She says she likes to make quilts for competition, and is looking

forward to the next AQS Show.

In her work, she always aims for perfection. Of her award she says, "Winning the AQS award gave me added incentive to keep striving for perfection, to keep in the competition. I went on to 'Delectable Pansies,' an applique quilt which won the National Quilting Association Best of Show and resulted in the Master Quilters Guild's awarding my quilt masterpiece status, the highest honor available through NQA."

Betty tells other quiltmakers to be sure to "enter shows where critique sheets are given. It is the most valuable, personal advice you can get to improve your quilting skills."

"When I look back on this quilt, I'm surprised I made it. For me it is a contemporary quilt. The rest of the 30 quilts I have completed are very traditional."

ISOMETRIC I
104" x 126"
1987
Betty Ekern
Suiter

Marla Hattabaugh
Scottsdale, Arizona

Varying Degrees

Marla Hattabaugh has been quilting since 1974 with various groups. After her first nephew was born, she says she made "the strangest Baby Blocks ever seen," and immediately "was hooked and started taking classes." Now a teacher herself, she says, "Beginning students are my greatest pleasure because they are so proud of their projects."

third place

1987 AQS Show & Contest
Innovative Pieced, Pro

Marla finds "much contrast in life (serious/funny; happy/sad; rich/poor)," and she includes it in her quilts. Talking about this award-winning quilt, she says, "I was enrolled in a self-discovery program at the time I was making it and was struck by the varying degrees of good that each person got out of the class. Making the circles different sizes indicated that idea. I still love to look at the quilt and enjoy the lines created by the stitching."

"This was an original design. Basically, there was a lot of strip piecing with some fiber manipulation. I'd seen a weaving using different designs and I wanted to do that with stitching." She continues, "As the quiltmaker, you can be in control of the quilting design. You can be as creative in that area as in selecting colors and shapes. I enjoy outlining some shapes and going 'against' other shapes and creating a different surface design." Looking at VARYING DEGREES, she adds, "Now I would add more lines."

Marla advises other quiltmakers "to do the best they can do and to keep at it. Trying new things is the way to learn – maybe not to succeed every time but to keep seeing new ways. I would also say that each judge is different and that each contest is different. Not winning is disheartening but not the end of the world – because there's always another show, and another chance. More important – make quilts because you love the process not because you may win a prize!"

"It is important for each and every quiltmaker to receive acknowledgment of some sort every once in a while. Because of the labor-intensive nature of our craft/art, we have a tendency to wonder if we are in the right field, so 'pats on the back' help to keep us centered and working to improve."

VARYING
DEGREES
76" x 86"
1986
Marla
Hattabaugh

Nathalie Chick
Wells, Maine

Shaded Grapes

Nathalie Chick says she likes the "graceful curves of flowers" and is "influenced by many things – nature, cloth, texture, color" when she designs her quilts. She has no formal art training, but her art teacher in high school said she had great ability. Remembering this teacher, Nathalie says, "She spent many hours after school showing me different

first place

1987 AQS Show & Contest Applique, Amateur

art methods." Nathalie has been quilting since 1979. Preferring to develop her own designs, Nathalie says she does not like using the patterns in quilt books.

To make this award-winning quilt, Nathalie used cloth left to her by her mother. She says she "could see the grapes in it even though it looked much different to other people." She used a fine bias method she learned from a book and then simplified.

Speaking of the development of the quilt Nathalie writes, "It took many hours of work, and I often got up at 4 a.m., worked for a couple of hours, and after a half hour's rest went back to work on it so that it could be finished for the "New England Images II" show. A bunch of grapes took 3 hours to applique, large leaves 1½

hours, long leaves 1½ hours and half leaves 55 minutes. In the border, two bars (2 in.) took a half hour."

In addition to the AQS show, this outstanding quilt has won several other awards.

Natalie says the quilt has brought many wonderful additions to her life; the response from people has been very rewarding. But she adds that there has been one disadvantage: "The disadvantage is that they now expect every quilt to be a winner."

Nathalie offers three pieces of advice to other quilters: "Do not be afraid to enter competitions. Be original and strive for perfection. Do not be reluctant to redo or change designs as you work on your project."

"The pleasure and pride of my husband, children and other family members has been very rewarding to me. The quilt has made me very popular with quilters and the public too. I have also been surprised by the number of men that have shown an interest in it."

SHADED
GRAPES
80" x 96"
1986
Nathalie Chick

Laverne N. Mathews
Orange, Texas

Strawberry Sundae

Laverne N. Mathews writes, "Making a strawberry quilt simmered in my mind for a year or two after seeing an antique quilt in the French Trading Post Museum in Beaumont, Texas, the colors so faded you could only imagine what they'd once been. A search of the literature yielded no exact pattern – not even strawberry quilt pictures. I would just have to

second place

*1987 AQS Show & Contest
Applique, Amateur*

design my own. A lovely drapery swatch gave me the perfect colors – pinkish-reds and greenish-blues running the gamut from pale to deep."

Speaking of the development of the design she continues, "The strawberry was drafted first, and then appliqued. How best to show them off? I used my flannel wall to arrive at a pleasing placement. What to put in the center? Folding and cutting paper finally gave the design

to be used there, taking one element from the strawberry. Now for a border that would link all the blocks and provide the frame."

Laverne was born in Wichita Falls, Texas, and grew up there and in East Texas. She says she is now retired, "after twenty-five years of teaching sixth and seventh graders to read and write more." She continues, "My husband loves quilts; my two sons like them, too. My two daughters-in-law even make quilts (we often collaborate), and my three grandchildren appreciate our output! What a great family! Traveling is a favorite pas-

time. The high desert country of Taos and Santa Fe, New Mexico claims us in the summer, where creative fires get replenished."

Laverne says she receives pleasure from looking at the picture of STRAWBERRY SUNDAE that hangs on her workroom wall. She adds, "I feel much like a proud parent, I guess. But actually the most exciting time for me (and most quiltmakers, I imagine) is when I am in the throes of creating."

"I have found out that an AQS award is BIG STUFF! And that having a quilt even in the show is considered quite a plum. Actually, of course, I feel no different, and it surprises me still when someone mentions it, and I'm held up as a quilting paragon."

To other quiltmakers Laverne says: "Make time for your creative endeavors, whatever avenue they take. Make space for them. Learn everything you can about them. Practice your art. Get better at it. Challenge yourself by competing. And trust your intuitive reactions."

"It was a long-ago artist who made a quilt that was the impetus for this present-day person's creative urge, thereby achieving a tiny bit of immortality. (Is this part of the charm of quiltmaking?) It seems most of my inspiration comes from the artists of days gone by."

STRAWBERRY
SUNDAE
70" x 84"
1986
Laverne N.
Mathews

Museum of AQS Collection

Mary R. Johnson
Munster, Indiana

Bird Of Paradise

Mary R. Johnson writes, "I taught myself to quilt after seeing the lovely quilts at the 1945 Lake County Fair in Crown Point, Indiana. The first quilt I made was a Double Wedding Ring. I made four more quilts in the next three years and then set quilting aside until 1974, when I began a bicentennial eagle quilt. Since that time I have made about 30 quilts, some

third place

*1987 AQS Show & Contest
Applique, Amateur*

patchwork, some applique. In the past few years. I have concentrated on applique. I love the freedom to improvise both pattern and color. I have participated in numerous competitions and shows and have won awards for my work.

The design of this quilt, Mary tells us, "is a copy of an applique album quilt top, c.1858-1863, as pictured in *Treasury of American Quilting*." She adds, "I first saw this quilt years ago in a magazine and always had in mind to make it. My daughter drew the patterns for me from the photograph in the book."

She continues, "I created my own color scheme, rather than following that of the original quilt. I used hundreds of different cotton materials in various colors and patterns to add texture and subtlety. I used reverse applique, small quilting patterns, and embroidery to enhance the details."

Asked what she would most like people to know about the quilt, Mary says, "the pleasure I got from mak-

ing each and every block – I love working with color – and the encouraging responses I got from my family, friends, and fellow quilters as they saw it take shape."

Speaking of her award she says, "It was a thrill to have my quilt accepted into the AQS show and to see it hanging along side so many beautiful and varied quilts. Receiving an award was the icing on a delicious cake!"

Mary's advice to other quiltmakers: "The joy of quilting is in the doing. Make what you like and find challenging. Trust your feelings, intuitions, and creativity – you will grow with each quilt. I would never make a quilt with the thought of winning an award, but I am *proud* of my work and I derive pleasure from seeing others respond to it, so I'm happy to enter shows and competitions, where I can share and exchange with other quilters."

"I still love the color, the animals, birds, objects and overall liveliness of the surface. And I continue to wonder about the original designer and how such a curious group of animals and birds came to be a part of this particular quilt design."

BIRD OF
PARADISE
78" x 93"
©1986
Mary R. Johnson

Velda Newman
Nevada City, California

Nasturtium

Velda Newman says that to create quilts like this award winner, she draws her patterns full-size on graph paper. She adds that she gathers ideas for these quilts from magazines, gardens, photographs, and seed catalogs.

Speaking of the materials and techniques used to create NASTURTIUM, Velda comments, "I like to use cotton or silk. If I can't find the right

first place

1987 AQS Show & Contest Applique, Pro

color, I dye it. I use controlled bleaching." She adds that once she has constructed the top, quilting is done in a free-form technique and is used as another design.

Velda was an art major in college and has sewn since a child. Of her background, she says, "Seven years ago I started quilting by making traditional pieced designs. I was not good at matching points. Then I found that I didn't have to do these traditional patterns – and if appliqueing, I didn't have to match the points. When I discovered that, I began to put all of my energy into quilting. When making original design applique quilts, I could do both my loves – sewing and art – at the same time." Velda lives in a small town, and says, "Entering competitions and attending shows is a way of being involved with other quilters."

Speaking of her AQS show experience, Velda says, "Quiltmaking for the most part is an individual effort. The consistent high caliber of the AQS Show, along with substantial cash awards, brings quiltmakers together. The competition enables quilters to see some of the best work available on a national level. It's nice to know that all those hours you spent alone on your quilt are appreciated."

"I consider color to be the most important element in quiltmaking. I recommend that quiltmakers keep trying to find the exact color, or improvise and make it." Thinking of her own sources for design, Velda also urges: "Be aware of your surroundings and keep a camera handy."

NASTURTIUM
89" x 96"
1987
Velda Newman

Dawn E. Amos
Rapid City, South Dakota

Between Two Worlds

Dawn E. Amos explains that she drew her own pattern for this award-winning quilt. She adds that with its bold color and abstract background, the piece is evidence of the influence Native American artist Oscar Howe has had on her work.

This quilt constructed with hand-dyed fabric was only the second appliqued quilt Dawn had made. Dawn

second place

1987 AQS Show & Contest Applique, Professional

adds, "This was my first experience using hand-dyed fabric and also my first experience working with 100% cotton. (The first applique quilt I made was a Statue of Liberty quilt for the Great American Quilt Festival in New York City – I used cotton/poly fabric for that.) I learned a lot. I had been making strictly star quilts for ten years or so, before I started developing my own designs."

Asked what she would like people to know about this quilt, Dawn replies, "I really like to leave the interpretation of my work up to the viewer. I like to let my work speak for me."

In response to a question about whether she feels differently now about the quilt than when she created it Dawn first says, "I hope I've gotten better!" and then adds, "I want to keep improving, making each one better that the last."

Speaking to other quilt-makers, Dawn says, "Do enter! And do go to these shows. There is a lot of talent out there, and there are a lot of great ones to learn from."

"This was the first year I entered the AQS show, and I had never taken a quilting class or anything. The most important part for me was knowing that I did have a chance, and could compete. My work has improved by being associated with other quilters at the top of their field. The quality of my work goes up with the quality of work around me."

BETWEEN
TWO WORLDS
70" x 80"
1987
Dawn E. Amos

Lyn Piercy
San Francisco, California

Kilauea Fire

Lyn Piercy developed this original, Hawaiian style design while Kilauea volcano was erupting. She "visualized the flames and fingers of flowing red-hot lava."

Lyn says she conceived a rough idea of the design while in the hospital after having surgery for breast cancer. The two colors used in the quilt are actually the front and back of one piece of fabric. Lyn adds that the streaky look of the mahogany red was not something she

third place

1987 AQS Show & Contest
Applique, Professional

had to add to the fabric; this 100% cotton was purchased with that look.

A renal dietitian for the University of California, Lyn is a self-taught quilter, but has a strong background in home sewing and clothing construction. She says, "Quilting has been my prime interest for about 15 years. I teach fine hand quilting and Hawaiian applique. My husband, Bill, and four adult children have been very supportive – especially since they see that my work can consistently win awards."

About winning the prize, Lyn says, "The award was a validation of the excellence of the quilt and of the time

spent in quilt endeavors."

Speaking to others who make quilts and enter them in competitions, Lyn suggests: "If you don't win one competition try another...and another. Competition and judges are different."

Unlike in traditional Hawaiian applique, where the whole top is cut and then basted, the design for KILAUEA FIRE was marked on the top, the top and background were basted together, and then the design was cut away and appliqued a little at a time.

KILAUEA FIRE
88" x 108"
1986
Lyn Piercy

Doris Welton
Plymouth, Michigan

Candlewick

Doris Welton explains that the candlewicking and embroidery on the individual blocks was done with crochet cotton. The scalloped edge has a small lace on it. She says, "The quilting pattern came to me as I worked on it." She then adds, "My husband does help with suggestions on the quilting patterns."

About her background Doris says, "I am 55 years old, have three married children and five grandchildren, and a husband that encourages me with quilting. I was raised in the country on the farm, but all of my married life has been lived in the city.

first place

*1987 AQS Show & Contest
Other Techniques, Ama*

I have always enjoyed sewing for family and friends, so it was rather natural to enjoy quilting. I just wish I had started it sooner."

Asked what she would most like people to know about her quilt, Doris replies, "This was my first quilt. The block patterns were taken from different quilt patterns, but the quilting pattern is original. It was made for a guest room."

Talking about her feelings about the quilt, Doris comments, "I was always happy with the end results – I had no experience with quilts before, and then to have people with knowledge in that field select it for first place. It will always be very special to me."

Commenting on her AQS show experience, Doris says, "I am always looking for the next quilt to start, but have enough patterns and ideas (in my head) to keep me busy for years. Friends bring me pictures of quilts and ideas. To other quiltmakers, Doris suggests, "Make what will give you satisfaction, (colors, material, patterns) and you usually will be happy with the finished product, even if it should never place in competition."

"It is now an annual trip for our family to go to the AQS Show & Contest; our married children go with us, and my mother. The men fish, while we ladies enjoy the quilt show; it's a great time for the family. Had I not won that first year, I probably would not enjoy the show as much as I do now."

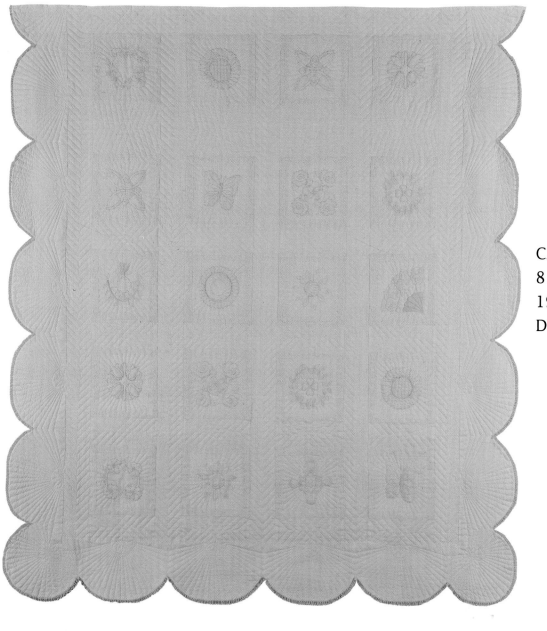

CANDLEWICK
81" x 93"
1986
Doris Welton

Mary Rushing
Tyler, Texas

3-D Pine Tree

Mary Rushing says she "used Janice Streeter's award-winning 3-D Pine Tree design" for this quilt which is pieced and appliqued. She constructed the quilt in all-cotton material: off-white muslin and blue and burgundy prints. Mary continues, "The prairie points are set in strips to give the three-dimensional effect. I used the quilting design that was

second place

*1987 AQS Show & Contest
Other Techniques, Ama*

included in the pattern. It is all hand quilted."

Mary would especially like people to know: "That there are 1,568 folded prairie points in this quilt. That it took patience and so many hours to make it that I lost count of the time, but by working most days and into the night, I finished it in 11 months. This was my 3rd quilt to make."

Born in Lafayette, Texas, Mary married James W. Rushing in 1945, in Tyler, Texas, and subsequently attended Abilene Christian College.

She is the mother of three daughters, and has 8 grandchildren. She moved from Houston, Texas, to Virginia Beach, Virginia, in 1959, and continued to reside there until July, 1988, when she returned to Texas following her husband's retirement. She now lives in Tyler, Texas. She comments, "I enjoy church work, sewing and quilting, which I began in 1984. Quilting is now in abeyance, however, because of after-effects of a broken right wrist suffered in April, 1989."

Asked if she feels any differently about 3-D PINE TREE now, she says, "Yes, because I was tired of it by the time I had finished. Now I like and appreciate it more each day. It is such a thrill when friends and neighbors come by to see it on the bed and then later call to see if they can bring their friends by. They all seem to admire it so much."

Of her award, Mary says, "I had made two quilts before this one and they had both been accepted for the AQS show in 1985 and 1986 and have won other awards which has been such a thrill and I felt so lucky. But to win second place for my 3rd one at

"Try to be as accurate as possible with every phase of your quilt. If it doesn't look right, take it out and start over."

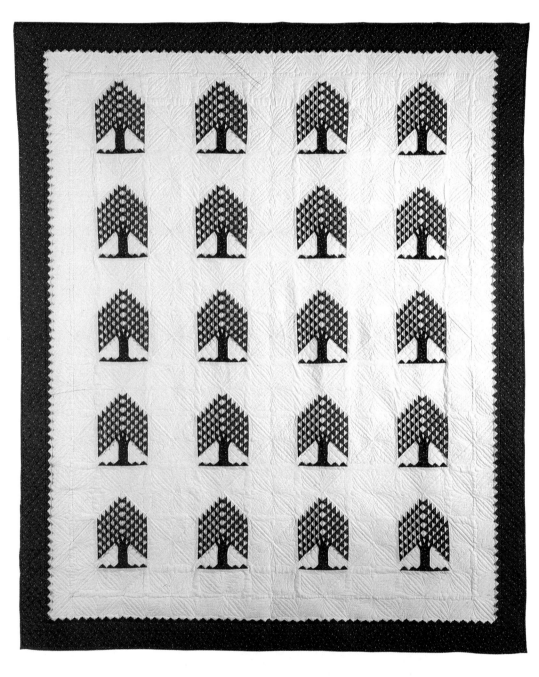

3-D
PINE TREE
86" x 103"
1986
Mary Rushing

the AQS show was one of the greatest thrills of my life. It gave me the confidence to send it to other shows for judging. It has won awards in five other shows including Best of Show in the Quilters Guild of East Texas in 1990."

Doris Amiss Rabey
Hyattsville, Maryland

A Dream In White

Doris Amiss Rabey says of quiltmaking, "I think with each quilt, you grow in knowledge, in design and for me, in patience." She continues, "This quilt was difficult for me, but perserverence paid off."

She says she has always "loved the look of white on white and the beautiful designs used." The design for this quilt is original. It was, in fact, her first design attempt, and she says it was "...almost

third place

*1987 AQS Show & Contest
Other Techniques, Ama*

left by wayside." She explains further, "I first put the design on silk pongee, tracing it wrong for the grain line. I rewashed and retraced it, only to find that after much, much work, I could not get a needle through the three layers. A year or more later I decided to try again and remarked the design on white cotton."

She combined the cotton top with a cotton backing and poly fill traditional batting and then used close quilting to enhance the overall design. The final results were this award-winning quilt. She says she feels "especially close" to

this quilt, "having spent so much time and effort on it – plus winning the award."

Doris has been quilting since 1973. She has won awards for her blocks and quilts, and has had several featured in magazines and quilt engagement calendars. She says she has had "no formal art training and was most pleased with the finished quilt design." She adds, "This original work inspired me to try designing in other areas as well."

Her advice to other quiltmakers: "Try and try again - who knows, you might be a prizewinner!"

"I began quilting in 1973. I inherited two tops I wanted to finish, joined the National Quilting Association to learn, won a ribbon in my first show (1974) and have been making quilts ever since then!"

A DREAM
IN WHITE
86" x 94"
1987
Doris Amiss
Rabey

Pat Denaxas
Mt. Prospect, Illinois

Garden Nouveau

No commercial patterns were used for this original-design quilt by Pat Denaxas, which was inspired by her interest in the Art Nouveau style, as found in printing, stained glass and poster art.

To make this stunning quilt, Pat used a combination of hand piecing and regular and reverse applique. She then embellished the design with embroidery and hand

first place

1987 AQS Show & Contest
Other Techniques, Pro

quilting, which she executed using traditional methods.

Pat has enjoyed many interests, including activities as different as being an ice skating instructor and being a landscape painting enthusiast. She began quilting "after admiring a friend's collection of antique quilts." She adds that she has "very little formal instruction in sewing." Her instruction has really involved just a few workshops, primarily in design.

Looking back at the quilt, she continues, "I'm still

proud of my quilt, but aware of things I could have done better. Quilting is always a learning and a growing experience."

She says that after winning the award, she "was invited to lecture at local quilt guilds and exhibit in several shows." She continues, "Winning has given me confidence to continue to

create quilts and enter them in competition. Unfortunately my work schedule and the hand construction I prefer limit my production."

When asked to offer advice to other quiltmakers, Pat says, "Don't skimp on the basics – good sewing techniques and careful planning are essential – but don't be afraid to make mistakes!"

"The quilt gave me a great deal of pleasure to create and encouraged me to research an art style I was interested in but had previously known little about. It was a constant learning experience!"

GARDEN
NOUVEAU
75" x 92"
1987
Pat Denaxas

Linda Goodmon Emery
Derby, Kansas

Persian Paisley

Oriental carpets and a paisley fabric Linda Goodmon Emery had cherished for several years were the inspiration for this award-winning quilt. A variety of cottons – ranging from antique fabrics to English pima cotton – and a variety of techniques – applique, layered applique, reverse applique, *broderie perse*, and bias banding – were used to create this hand-

second place

1987 AQS Show & Contest Other Techniques, Pro

sewn and hand-quilted work.

Of the quilt, Linda says, "I wanted it to have the feeling of an Oriental carpet. Since I am not knowledgeable about Oriental carpets (other than admiring them), I did extensive research before beginning the design. I began with over 100 possible fabrics to use in the quilt and kept eliminating them as I worked. This quilt is more complex than it appears. For example, there are nine strips sewn together for the outside borders. The quilting is hardly visible on the front, even though I quilted this one to death! You have to look at the back to see the quilting."

Linda has been a quilter since 1975 and specializes in original design quilts of all sizes and techniques. Her quilts have won numerous awards, and she is a National Quilting Association Master Quilter, and the author of *A Treasury of Quilting Designs* (AQS, 1990). She also teaches, lectures and designs patterns.

Speaking about PERSIAN PAISLEY, Linda says, "This quilt was my favorite when I made it and it remains so. This quilt gives me so much enjoyment it would take a super-spectacular quilt to top it. I make my quilts to try out new techniques, explore designs. They are made to please me, but it is so gratifying when others like them too."

She encourages other quiltmakers to do the same: "Make your quilts to please yourself and don't be influenced by the current design and color trends that are the most popular. If you have a spark of an idea, build on it and make it grow. Let your quilts reflect you."

"Winning is great but is totally unpredictable. Your quilt may be spectacular and not win a ribbon. Don't give up; enter it in other shows; try even harder with your next quilt, but don't ever quit."

PERSIAN
PAISLEY
70" x 87"
©1987
Linda Goodmon
Emery

Joan Schulze
Sunnyvale, California

Earthquake Country

Joan Schulze explains, "EARTHQUAKE COUNTRY is based on a block I designed in 1979 and freely interpreted to suggest landscape in my area, near the San Andreas Fault. I wanted to suggest the surface calm on a warm sunny day."

To construct the quilt, Joan used her dyed and painted silk and cotton. She

third place

1987 AQS Show & Contest
Other Techniques, Pro

machine and hand pieced, appliqued and hand quilted the work.

Born in Chicago, Illinois, Joan has been a free-lance studio artist since 1970, and a quiltmaker since 1974. Her work has been exhibited in museums and galleries in United States, England, Japan and Eastern and Western Europe. Her work has been featured in many publications. She has taught across the United States and in Canada and was a visiting artist for five months in Australia in 1984 and 1989.

Asked about the effect of her AQS show award experience, Joan comments, "It is always appreciated to get one's work validated, and helps when things aren't going so well."

To other quiltmakers Joan says, "Make your quilts to please yourself. If they please others, that's a bonus. Keep competitions in perspective. They are not reasons to make quilts as it prevents the joy of making something wonderful."

"This quilt is part of a series based on where I live, dealing especially with earthquakes. I think it is more poignant since our October 1989 earthquake, which has changed so much of the area I used for the design."

EARTHQUAKE
COUNTRY
74" x 85"
©1986
Joan Schulze

Julee Prose
Ottumwa, Iowa

Community Barn Raising

Julee Prose's award-winning quilt COMMUNITY BARN RAISING is a variation of the traditional Log Cabin block. Julee explains, "The blocks are set in the Barn Raising pattern – I added appliqued borders using Amish buggies winding through the country side. All of this gives the quilt its title."

She continues, "The majority of the blocks are machine-pieced. I drafted my

first place

*1987 AQS Show & Contest
Theme: Log Cabin*

border full-size, using blank newspaper (end rolls purchased from a local newspaper). I made two copies of each border, one for pattern, one for cutting. I numbered each piece before cutting, then appliqued all pieces. I quilted in the ditch in the blocks and used contour quilting in borders."

About her background, Julee says, "I am married (Paul), have a son (Robert) and one Himalayan cat (Billie). I am currently manager at a portrait studio. I'm still quilting and entering contests." She adds, "I've gotten freer with my designs. I'm such a

traditionalist! I'm using more variety in fabric and colors."

Asked if she now feels the same way about COMMUNITY BARN RAISING as she did when she made it, Julee replies, "No – it is not my favorite quilt, probably because it is so dark. I've sold most of my works but managed to keep a couple of them, one is my Blue Delft (1985 AQS Show) and red/tan Oak Leaf. I feel that these are my best workmanship quilts and my favorites – they will

be kept as family heirlooms."

About her AQS show experience Julee says, "I've met a lot of different people. You definitely have more notoriety. I enjoy the challenge of each contest."

To other quiltmakers, Julee says, "Keep trying! the judges' critiques help you improve your skills. I always look forward to seeing the judges' cards." She adds, "Before sending a quilt for a contest, always use a lint brush on both sides."

"Sometimes the simplest of quilt designs can be winners – quilts don't always have to be intricate in design to win."

COMMUNITY
BARN RAISING
78" x 102"
1987
Julee Prose

Museum of AQS Collection

Hallie H. O'Kelley
Tuscaloosa, Alabama

Zinnias In The Windows Of My Log Cabin

Hallie O'Kelley says, "This was an original concept using the Log Cabin design surrounding the square, with a zinnia flower in the square. Each summer we grow in our yard zinnias of assorted colors, which make a stunning bouquet when used together. It was this picture of color that I wanted to portray in the quilt."

Speaking of the develop-

second place

1987 AQS Show & Contest Theme: Log Cabin

ment of the quilt, Hallie adds, "The fabric used was 100% cotton which had either been hand-dyed (the green logs) or screen-printed (the flowers). The quilt was constructed by machine piecing and hand quilting. I always use the lap quilting technique, but without a hoop or other frame."

About her background, Hallie says, "I have a master's degree in applied art from Iowa State University, with a major in textile design. My medium is silk-screen printing, and for a number of years I have been hand printing greeting cards and posters. I have been quilting since 1981 when I first tried out an idea that had been developing in my mind. That idea was to design and screen print fabric to simulate an appliqued quilt. Since that time, I have refined the technique and use hand-printed fabrics along with hand-dyed ones."

In regards to ZINNIAS IN THE WINDOWS OF MY LOG CABIN, Hallie says, "I would like people to know that this is an original idea, even though it is based on a tradi-

tional design." She continues, "I can't say that I feel any differently about the quilt now than when I made it. Perhaps this is because I only had the quilt in my home for a few months. It was completed just in time to enter the AQS show. Then, a couple of months after it returned from this show, the American Quilter's Society bought it for their collection. Since then I have only seen its picture. I am proud, however, to have it in that collection."

"Winning an award on a quilt in a show of the high caliber of the AQS show is certain to have an effect on a quilter's life," says Hallie. "It gave a boost to my ego, as well as affirmed that I was going the right way with my quilting. It also gave me a feeling of self-confidence in what I was doing."

In her advice to other quiltmakers, Hallie says, "If you feel that you have made a beautiful quilt, don't be afraid to enter it in competition. You can learn from sharing it with others."

"I would urge other quiltmakers to try to use some originality when making a quilt. Don't make it just like one you have admired that someone else has made, but add your own personal touch to it. Let the quilt you have admired just be the starting point for planning your quilt."

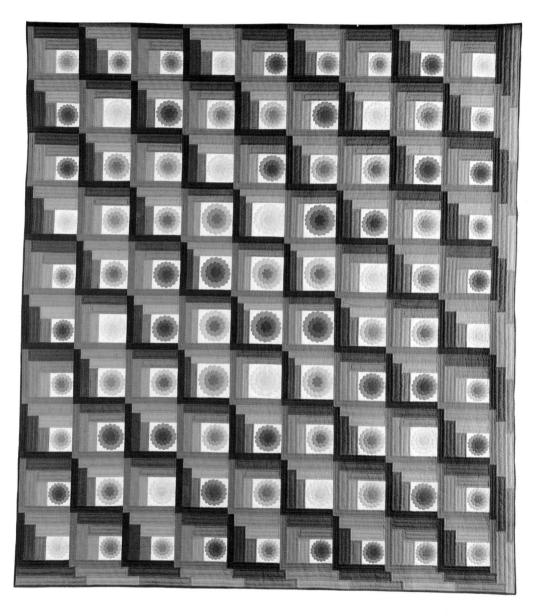

ZINNIAS
IN THE
WINDOWS
OF MY
LOG CABIN
77" x 85"
©1987
Hallie H. O'Kelley

Museum of AQS Collection

Ruth Britton Smalley
Houston, Texas

Square Within A Square Within A Square

Ruth Britton Smalley used 100 different cotton fabrics in this machine-pieced, hand-quilted quilt using Log Cabin blocks set in the Barn Raising pattern. Ruth explains, "SQUARE WITHIN A SQUARE WITHIN A SQUARE was totally unplanned. I simply collected numerous fabrics which I liked together and divided them in darks and lights and then the fun began. The

third place

1987 AQS Show & Contest Theme: Log Cabin

choices of colors changed with each additional strip. There are no two blocks alike."

Of her background, Ruth explains, "I began quilting in 1984 (not counting a boring Cathedral Window quilt I started in 1973 and never finished). My interest was aroused by the books on contemporary quilt artists and the Amish. I painted for a number of years and worked in jewelry, metal work and wood sculpture (Nevelson style). I think of a quilt as a painting whether it is graphic or non-objective. All the same elements of art are involved in designing a quilt – line, color, shape, tone, texture. My B.S. was in interior decoration at Texas Women's University."

"SQUARE WITHIN A SQUARE WITHIN A SQUARE was my first completed quilt, and winning a ribbon gave me tremendous encouragement and inspiration to keep exploring the possibilities which are unending. My philosophy is that anything worth doing is worth doing well. My husband and I travel a great deal and my fabric collection grows with each trip, especially in foreign countries such as Egypt, Russia, China, Japan, India, South Africa, England, Germany, Italy, France, Finland, Bali and Singapore. At the present time I am working on a series of contemporary pieces. My life-long interest in painting, sewing, sculpture, jewelry and metalwork are all coming together as a summary of my entire life experiences."

Ruth continues, "Creativity for me is a spontaneous pouring out of impressions, moods, sensations, energy

"I still am pleased with the quilt. It is always an adventure to feast my eyes on the constantly changing colors. You see the same thing happening in nature, which is the basis for my inspiration."

SQUARE
WITHIN
A SQUARE
WITHIN
A SQUARE
102" x 102"
1986
Ruth Britton
Smalley

and vitality. Quilts are a form of art and since I've always been interested in pursuing various forms of art, making quilts seems to be the right medium for me to continue my interests. The collage is of utmost importance to me at this time. The spontaneity is stifled if rigid patterns are set. I prefer to simply start the action by cutting shapes and letting the motion created by the various shapes carry me on to the next step and on to the next quilt. I see my audience as myself, people and jurors. It is a great personal joy to get a good response from my quilts. My desire is to make quilts that will involve and interest others – to communicate."

Sandra Heyman, Burns, Kansas
Linda Nonken, El Dorado, Kansas

Hot Stuff

Sandra Heyman and Linda Nonken comment, "After the rose quilt (a winner in the 1986 AQS Show), we felt a need for a different style of design and work." For this award-winning quilt, they developed an original design involving "hexagons and various parts thereof." This quilt is constructed of 100% cotton fabric with a polyester batting and a printed backing.

first place

1987 AQS Show & Contest Group/Team

Sandra is a master wheat weaver and has since 1976 been an exhibitor at War Eagle Farm in Arkansas. Linda has done alterations professionally since 1977 and is currently producing a line of folk jewelry and dolls. Sandra is making miniature quilts from feed sacks. Both have done needlework and sewing since early childhood. This shared effort began on a shopping trip in 1983. Sandra mentioned an antique bed for which she wanted a quilt. Linda said, "I'll help you," and the partnership began. Linda lives near El Dorado, Kansas, and Sandra lives near Burns, Kansas, and their families have been friends for many years.

Speaking of the quilt Sandra and Linda explain, "Our purpose was to create a piece with color gradation. Originally the color scheme was to be different but those colors were not available commercially." They add, "We have enjoyed various commentaries about the source of light in the center of the quilt and speculation about fabric content."

Sandra and Linda add that they used the English piecing method and hand quilting to complete the quilt.

Sandra and Linda began working together as quiltmakers in 1983. As a team, they have constructed eleven major quilts, two of which have been Sweepstakes winners at the Kansas State Fair (1984 and 1986). They have also won ribbons and Viewer's Choice awards at many other judged shows, and their quilts have been featured in various quilting magazines and calendars.

210

"The opportunity to be able to compete on this level and then to place is very gratifying. It is always encouraging when so many people have read the magazines and comment on having seen our quilts pictured."

HOT STUFF
88" x 99"
©1986
Sandra Heyman
& Linda Nonken

To other quiltmakers, Sandra and Linda recommend: "Do your very best on each quilt because you may want to enter a contest with it some day. You refine and hone your work on each of your quilts if you make them for competition. There is always a place for each quilt in a show somewhere. Don't give up with one rejection."

Joyce Kassner, Toni Smith & Susan Somerlath
Chesterfield, Missouri

Pennsylvania Dutch Folk Art

Joyce Kassner doesn't design quilts but likes to work with original designs, so she often calls on her friends for assistance. About this award-winning quilt Joyce says, "Susan Somerlath developed the design in conjunction with a class she was teaching. She started in the center, and then added borders out."

Joyce Kassner says that

second place

1987 AQS Show & Contest Team/Group

when she first saw Susan's design, she thought she'd never be able to make a quilt like that. Gradually, though, she developed the skills, and then tackled the design, asking another friend, Toni Smith, to do the quilting. Joyce comments that her "group" is a little different from the usual – Susan and Toni have never even met each other!

Joyce started quilting in 1980 – she explains that she began tole painting, photography and quilting at the same time. She adds, "Quilting won out. I don't even know how to load the film in my camera and have no tole painting left, but my fabric collection is substantial." She continues, "I taught for a while in a shop, and have maintained many quilting friendships from there. It's wonderful therapy."

Joyce says she most likes to make quilts which combine applique and piecing. She likes to do both, and feels that the combination adds interest to the designs – it also doesn't get so boring.

Asked if the award has had a great effect on her life or her quilting, Joyce comments, "The award hasn't made much of a difference." She adds, "It's always fun to win, though, to enter and see how your work rates with peers."

Her advice to others making quilts: JUST DO IT! She adds that it is hard for her to give other people advice. She really enjoys making quilts, but realizes that some enjoy it and some don't.

Joyce Kassner: "Someone I'd sold a number of my quilts to wanted this one, but I couldn't part with it. It is the first really difficult challenge I had made – it's like one of my kids – I couldn't give it up."

PENNSYLVANIA
DUTCH FOLK
ART
92" X 92"
1987
Joyce Kassner

Designed by
Susan
Somerlath
Quilted by Toni
Smith

Palouse Hills

Ellen Arnold, current president of the Palouse Patchers, explains that the design of PALOUSE HILLS was "influenced by the countryside around Moscow, the fields. The border represents the wheat and the dry peas

third place

1987 AQS Show & Contest
Group/Team

produced here."

"The detailing work," says Ellen, "was done by Shirley Nilsson, with her technique of machine stitching. The rest was hand quilted by members of the club." Ellen adds, "The hills were designed using a flexible curve."

Ellen explains "The quilt was originally made as a raffle quilt for our annual quilt show. It turned out so great

we decided to keep it for the club to share with the community and other quilters who would appreciate it."

Ellen says the group does not feel any differently about the quilt now than when it was first completed. She explains, "Our club continues to be proud of our PALOUSE HILLS quilt – it is our 'flagship' quilt and we are eager to share it with other groups and shows!"

*Ellen Arnold: "This quilt proves a group can develop a piece of art –
perhaps this is an example that quilters depend on one another
for inspiration – when one succeeds we all succeed!"*

PALOUSE HILLS
58" x 82"
1986
Palouse Patchers

Linda S. Perry
Lexington, Massachusetts

Berkeley Blue

Linda S. Perry says of her quilt, "BERKELEY BLUE is my original design influenced by my love of Japanese design." She adds that cottons, silks and wools (including contemporary and antique Japanese fabrics), as well as hand-dyed and hand-painted fabrics, were used in this machine-pieced, hand-appliqued, and machine-quilted quilt.

Of her background, Linda says, "In 1983 I was home with

first place

1987 AQS Show & Contest Wall Quilt, Amateur

my infant son, on leave from teaching high school mathematics. That year I saw my first art quilts. I thought they were spectacular! The sense of light in Linda Levin's quilts and the mathematical complexity of Ruth McDowell's appealed to me enormously. It was the excitement of coming home. While my background is in mathematics, I had taken numerous art courses and had worked as a scientific illustrator. Ever since I can remember I have loved fabric. When I found art quilts I felt I had found my medium. Just going into a fabric store makes my heart beat faster. What's so satisfying about quilting is that you can buy an ⅛ yard of some totally outrageous fabric and do something with it."

"My work is influenced by my love of Art Deco and Japanese design. I have learned about art from numerous teachers and friends, the most significant being Albert Alcalay at Harvard University. In his own words, he taught by 'contamination': and, indeed, his enthusiasm was infectious. Besides quilting, I am the mother of one boy, Luke Daniel. I love to read, I ski tolerably well and my husband and I enjoy an absolutely wretched game of badminton. On occasion I love composing fancy dinners, sit down dinners with five or six courses

and at least two desserts. I cannot abide following a recipe. I cook by feel, balancing taste and texture and colors. This is how I quilt."

"I made this quilt right after taking a design course at Harvard. As I worked on it, I tried to incorporate what had been taught about color and design. It was gratifying to see newly acquired skills taking tangible form as this quilt evolved. When I compare BERKELEY BLUE to my previous quilts, I am pleased to see how far I came. At the time I made it, I felt that BERKELEY BLUE was a major turning point for me. I still do."

Concerning her AQS award, Linda comments, "Winning a first prize at the AQS show has had a long lasting effect on me. I am honored to receive this award from such a highly regarded panel of judges. This recognition gives me a sense of validation and strengthens my resolve to make art quilts as a full-time occupation.

Linda says, "My advice to other quilters is: Keep making quilts! If you get stuck, start another one. You only have momentum when you are working. One quilt leads to another. Staying stuck leads nowhere. Keep making quilts."

"When I see that plaque on the wall I feel reassured that I am not going off the deep end as I cut up material and then sew it back together."

BERKELEY
BLUE
38" x 55½"
©1986
Linda S. Perry

Catherine M. Jordan
Granite Springs, New York

Swans On The Mill Pond

Catherine M. Jordan's husband, John A. Jordan writes, "Catherine Jordan passed away in November, 1987. She had fought Hodgkin's disease for 15 years. When she went to Paducah for the show in 1987, she was a very sick but determined lady. I'm amazed that she had the strength to do it. She returned from Paducah and returned to the hospital. Quilting helped her

second place

1987 AQS Show & Contest Wall Quilt, Amateur

maintain her sanity over a long ordeal – it became her reason for continuing."

Catherine was the mother of four children and a nurse by training. In her interview with *American Quilter* magazine editors at the 1987 show, she explained that SWANS ON THE MILL POND had been inspired by the applique of Jo Diggs. She described how she sketched the scene, gathered fabrics, and then constructed the quilt section by section. She said the quilt "went together beautifully," and added that many of the good design considerations happened by accident. She commented, "Even though this quilt kept on growing and growing, I just had a wonderful time doing it."

Catherine's artist friends found the focus of the quilt exquisite – she brought people in at the left and they then followed the road up to the sun, the birds, the mountains and to the start of a new day.

218

John A. Jordan about Catherine M. Jordan: "Quilting helped her maintain her sanity over a long ordeal – it became her reason for continuing."

SWANS ON THE
MILL POND
48" x 48"
©1986
Catherine M.
Jordan

Virginia Ferrill Piland
Berea, Kentucky

The Gilgamesh Tapestry

Virginia Ferrill Piland explains, "When I decided to make THE GILGAMESH TAPESTRY, I had already been interested in Sumerian culture for several years, particularly in the Gilgamesh epic, the oldest story known to man, dating back to 3000 years B.C. Because I wanted the hanging to be as archaeologically accurate as possible, I studied at the University of

third place

1987 AQS Show & Contest Wall Quilt, Amateur

Chicago Oriental Institute. From the start, I wanted to create a piece which might someday find its proper place at Berea College, my alma mater."

"It is made in five registers, the top and bottom registers showing parades of people, an idea adapted from the Standard of Ur, one of the most famous artifacts from Mesopotamia (present-day Iraq). Basing figures on other artifacts, I added other registers to show the gods and significant events in the life of Gilgamesh, and the develop-

ment of written language from pictograph to cuneiform."

Virginia continues, "I have been asked if I first drafted the entire hanging and then proceeded with the work. Good Heavens No! I first made one figure to determine that I could indeed create an authentic look. Then, much like the archaeologist who digs up first one and then another shard and then reconstructs a piece of pottery, I designed and made each figure separately until I had enough for an entire register. Friends helped in finding desert-colored, suitably

textured fabrics. Real jewelry and three-dimensional objects were used where appropriate."

"Making this quilt," Virginia adds, "has had a profound influence on me. One cannot sit for 2,000 hours at the task and not become immersed in the ancient culture. This quilt has brought me into contact with recognized authorities of Sumerian culture. People from as far away as Saudi Arabia have written me about it. This, of course, is very gratifying. More importantly, not only have my eyes been opened to that culture, but I now view my own present-day world in a different light. Almost daily, I have reminders of our indebtedness to Sumer, that land known as the Cradle of Civilization."

Virgina comments, "Perhaps the thing I am most proud of is that it now hangs at the entrance of the Berea College Library. It has been used on occasion by members of the philosophy and the astronomy departments as a 'reference book.' I had never planned to write a textbook." Asked about her background, Virginia says, "There was no

"Now that the quilt is safely hanging in the Berea College Library in a cherry frame and plexiglass, I will reveal a secret. A message is buried in the walls of the hanging. Some future archaeologist, when this piece begins to decay, might unearth that message."

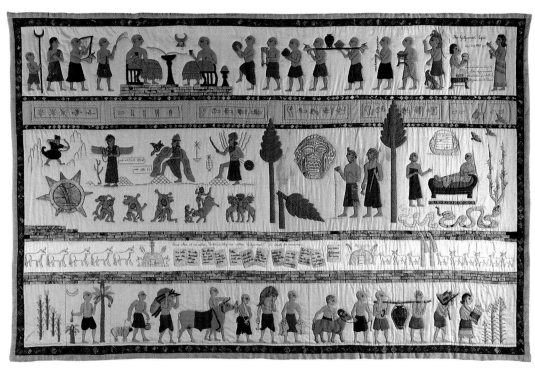

THE GILGAMESH
TAPESTRY
96" x 60"
1986
Virginia Ferrill
Piland

tradition of quilting in my family. I cannot recall ever having seen a quilting frame set up until I set up my own in 1975. Much of my childhood was spent in chasing butterflies and searching for dinosaur eggs. Only recently, when I located a letter to Santa Claus asking for a sewing kit, did I remember having been interested in sewing. Prior to making THE GILGAMESH TAPESTRY, I had made a few applique quilts; some of them award winners.

At one point when I had worked myself to exhaustion to meet a show deadline, I decided to make a more serious piece, and the seed for THE GILGAMESH TAPESTRY was planted.

Virginia adds, "Professionally, I have been a psychologist, an elementary teacher, and a junior high school teacher of English and literature. I am now retired, but I have not yet located that rocking chair for the front porch."

Charlotte Warr Andersen
Kearns, Utah

Three For The Crown

Charlotte Warr Andersen says THREE FOR THE CROWN "is a tribute to the Triple Crown of horse racing – the beauty and fluidity of thoroughbred horses. She comments, "In it, I tried to incorporate many aspects that memorialize the races – the traditions, the histories, the excitement, the crowds. I did a lot of research." Charlotte adds that she would like peo-

first place

1987 AQS Show & Contest Wall Quilt, Professional

ple to know that "the horses are *pieced* not appliqued."

She continues, "The buildings and horses are my own design. The first in each series of 6" blocks is a Crown block. The other three blocks are state blocks from each of the states where the Triple Crown races are run. The border is Blazing Star from Jinny Beyer's book of blocks and borders."

The quilt is "made of cottons, poly-cotton blends, silks and one piece of rayon. All parts of the top of the quilt are hand-pieced except for the jockey's hands which

were too small and complicated to piece, and a few touches of embroidery. The piece is hand quilted."

Speaking of her background, Charlotte says, "I have been making quilts since 1974, and decided to make it my profession in 1983. I specialize in one-of-a-kind pictorial quilts ranging from abstract/representational to almost photographic reality. I have won numerous awards for my work."

Asked if she feels any differently about the quilt now, Charlotte replies, "No. I think about my quilts a long time

before I ever draw a line, cut any fabric or take a stitch. They develop and change while I'm thinking on the idea and then while I'm making it. When I'm done, the quilt is a complete statement and very rarely do I wish later that I'd done some little thing differently. I have no desire to do series quilts and this is probably why."

Asked to give advice to others, Charlotte says, "Quiltmakers of the past incorporated things that were important to them. Draw something out of your life that means something to you to put in your quilts."

222

"Be original. If you're making a traditional pattern give it an unusual treatment. If you're making a contemporary piece incorporate something contemporary from today's world."

THREE FOR
THE CROWN
54" x 54"
1987
Charlotte Warr
Andersen

Museum of AQS Collection

Laura Munson Reinstatler
Seattle, Washington

Fan Dance

Laura Munson Reinstatler explains that in this quilt, "The fan is strip-pieced, using approximately ¼ inch finished strips. The quilt was also slashed and ½ inch finished strips were added and, in some areas, woven to create an illusion of three-dimensionality. The fabrics are either 100% cottons or cotton/polyester blends. The quilt is machine pieced and

second place

1987 AQS Show & Contest Wall Quilt, Professional

quilted." She continues, "After I machine quilted, I brought all the threads to the back of the piece and tied them, then needle-wove the ends inside the quilt."

Laura Munson Reinstatler is a fiber artist and designer. She holds a B.A. in art with a textile emphasis which includes basic design, textile science, fiber processes, costume design and history. After working in costume design and construction for theatre, she apprenticed with weaver Jette Nevers in Denmark. Laura began quilting

ten years ago using strip-piecing techniques in wearable art. She began creating wall quilts in 1985, exploring color relationships, luminosity and three-dimensionality. She has participated extensively in juried and invitational exhibitions throughout the country, including the prestigious Fairfield/Concord Fashion Show. Her work has also appeared in many textile books and periodicals. Laura lectures and teaches, and recently co-authored *Artwear Jumper*, a pattern booklet. Her work is included in collections in the United States, Canada and Europe.

Laura would like people to know that "FAN DANCE was designed not only to be a pleasing arrangement of color and shape, but also to suggest the feeling of undulation and movement within a three-dimensional situation."

Describing her own reactions to the quilt, Laura says, "When I drew the design for the quilt, I was pleased with the idea. When working on the quilt (as often happens with my quilts), I tired of it, and began to question its

design validity, color choice, and craftsmanship. Upon its completion, I was sick of it! But after not seeing it for a long period of time (it was being exhibited out of the area), I lost the negative feeling about it and actually enjoyed seeing it again. Now I am able to enjoy it." Laura adds, "Being so intimately involved with a quilt during the creating process usually is a love-hate affair for me. Months or even years later I usually like the pieces I've done. It's almost like having unruly but loved children come back home again."

Asked about the effect of her AQS award, Laura says, "I'm not sure. I was shocked when it won, and, of course, thrilled. I almost never enter my quilts in competition. I don't know why. I guess they never seem quite good enough."

Her advice to other quilt-makers: "Do something you enjoy or love passionately, whether with color, or shape or texture, etc. Keep your eyes open! 'What if' a lot. Expose yourself to as much creative input as you can; whether it's books about

"One of the best pieces of advice I have ever heard about making quilts came from Jean Ray Laury. She said, 'Just make your next quilt.' I have derived great comfort from that statement, especially after being overwhelmed by the stunning quilts I see in exhibits and in publications. Sometimes I feel like giving up! But then I hear a little angel's voice, 'Just make your next quilt.' Thanks, Jean!"

FAN DANCE
52" x 52"
©1985
Laura Munson
Reinstatler

quilts, design, flowers, cooking; or lectures and workshops; or window shopping; or reading the newspapers; explore as much as you can. Do something creative every day. It doesn't have to be quilt-related.

Solveig Ronnqvist
Warwick, Rhode Island

Fields Of Plenty

Speaking of this original design, Solveig Ronnqvist says, "I wanted to continue exploring the use of perspective and the juxtaposition of a panoramic view with the detailed close-up of a portion of that view, which I had used as basis for my quilt "Distant Closeness," which was purchased for the Museum of the American Quilter's Society." She adds that this quilt is

third place

1987 AQS Show & Contest Wall Quilt, Professional

constructed of cotton fabrics and a cotton batting and is totally machine-pieced and machine-quilted.

About her background Solveig says, "Born and raised in Helsinki, Finland, I came to Hartford, Connecticut in 1965, after graduation from high school. In 1970, I received a B.S. degree in apparel designing/merchandising from the University of Connecticut. Upon moving to Rhode Island, I worked as store manager and associate buyer for several women's apparel stores until I opened a quilt shop in Wickford, Rhode Island, in 1976. The business and my interest in quilting grew from a part-time activity to a full-time occupation. In 1984, I sold the business to concentrate on the artistic aspects of quiltmaking and to design and wholesale patterns for quilters. Since 1978, I have exhibited work in solo exhibits, group shows, and galleries and have had work shown in several national publications. My work is included in private and corporate collections."

About FIELDS OF PLENTY, Solveig says she would like people to know, "This quilt is

also a more serious comment on the wealth and abundance we are so fortunate to enjoy in this country, a fact we sometimes lose sight of." Speaking of her own feelings about the quilt, she says, "As with much of my work, it was a marathon race to get the quilt completed in time for a solo exhibit. After its hectic completion, the quilt has been out of my hands, on exhibit, for most of the past four years. I look forward to its intermittent homecomings, like you do a grown child whom you raised and sent out into the world. I am proud of it and happy with the outcome, but keep working towards new goals and greater accomplishments."

Of the award Solveig says, "It was a great morale boost to be recognized for my work. The fact that it also entailed a monetary award helped to legitimize my efforts as a quilt artist. The quilt has since been exhibited all over this country and in several national quilt publications, resulting in much positive feedback and mail from as far as South Africa."

"Do the best work you can possibly do. Take pride in your accomplishments. Participating in juried shows gives you a healthy perspective on the quality of your own work and should be looked upon as a positive learning experience to improve your own skills."

FIELDS OF
PLENTY
74" x 60"
©1986
Solveig
Ronnqvist

Lucille Daley
Davis, Oklahoma

Run For The Roses

The colors in this quilt, Lucille Daley tells us, "came from the flowers and trees we would see coming down Interstate-57 and in the gardens of Paducah." Since the quilt was made especially for her daughter, who loves horses, Lucille named it RUN FOR THE ROSES.

The quilt is made of 100% cotton, except for batting, and has two borders of the

viewer's choice

1987 AQS Show & Contest

pieced work which is constructed of the "theme fabrics." The theme fabrics determine the colors that are used in the applique work.

Lucille tells us that she has "been a senior citizen for a long time." She continues, "Upon my retirement I took applique lessons from Nancy Pearson, and from these classes developed a strong friendship. Now I try to enter a quilt wherever Nancy is teaching. I love the curved shapes she uses in her patterns."

This particular quilt, uses

flowers from a Nancy Pearson pattern, and Lucille says it is one of her favorites. After winning the viewer award in Paducah, it has gone on to win many ribbons in other shows and is now widely recognized wherever it is shown.

Lucille says that the quilt has become a very special one for her. She explains, "It has been entered in so many

shows that I now feel it is a part of me. I have had offers to sell it, but cannot part with it. It was my first applique quilt."

About her show experience, Lucille comments, "I was surprised and happy that my quilt was accepted in the 1986 show. But having it selected by the viewers was a real thrill. I was told it won by a large margin."

"I would like to see more 'new names' entering the competition. It is such a thrill to see your quilt hung, and it motivates you to try again. Go for it!"

RUN FOR THE
ROSES
80" x 90"
1985
Lucille Daley

INDEX / QUILTMAKERS

INDEX / QUILTS

∼American Quilter's Society∽

dedicated to publishing books
for today's quilters

The following AQS publications are currently available:

American Beauties: Rose & Tulip Quilts
by Gwen Marston & Joe Cunningham
#1907: AQS, 1988, 96 pages, softbound, $14.95

America's Pictorial Quilts by Caron L. Mosey
#1662: AQS, 1985, 112 pages, hardbound, $19.95

Applique Designs: My Mother Taught Me to Sew
by Faye Anderson
#2121: AQS, 1990, 80 pages, softbound, $12.95

Arkansas Quilts: Arkansas Warmth
Arkansas Quilter's Guild, Inc.
#1908: AQS, 1987, 144 pages, hardbound, $24.95

Art of Hand Applique, The by Laura Lee Fritz
#2122: AQS, 1990, 80 pages, softbound, $14.95

...Ask Helen More About Quilting Designs by Helen Squire
#2099: AQS, 1990, 54 pages, 17 x 11, spiral-bound, $14.95

Classic Basket Quilts by Elizabeth Porter and Marianne Fons
#2208: AQS, 1991, 128 pages, softbound, $16.95

Collection of Favorite Quilts, A by Judy Florence
#2119 AQS, 1990, 136 pages, softbound, $18.95

Dear Helen, Can You Tell Me?
...all about quilting designs by Helen Squire
#1820: AQS, 1987, 56 pages, 17 x 11, spiral-bound, $12.95

Dyeing & Overdyeing of Cotton Fabrics by Judy Mercer Tescher
#2030: AQS, 1990, 54 pages, softbound, $9.95

Fun & Fancy Machine Quiltmaking by Lois Smith
#1982: AQS, 1989, 144 pages, softbound, $19.95

Gallery of American Quilts: 1849-1988
#1938: AQS, 1988, 128 pages, softbound, $19.95

Gallery of American Quilts 1860-1989: Book II
#2129: AQS, 1990, 128 pages, softbound, $19.95

The Grand Finale: A Quilter's Guide to Finishing Projects
by Linda Denner
#1924: AQS, 1988, 96 pages, softbound, $14.95

Heirloom Miniatures by Tina M. Gravatt
#2097: AQS, 1990, 64 pages, softbound, $9.95

Home Study Course in Quiltmaking
by Jeannie M. Spears
#2031: AQS, 1990, 240 pages, softbound, $19.95

Ins and Outs, The: Perfecting the Quilting Stitch
by Patricia J. Morris
#2120: AQS, 1990, 96 pages, softbound, $9.95

Irish Chain Quilts: A Workbook of Irish Chains & Related Patterns
by Joyce B. Peaden
#1906: AQS, 1988, 96 pages, softbound, $14.95

Marbling Fabrics for Quilts: A Guide for Learning & Teaching
by Kathy Fawcett and Carol Shoaf
#2206: AQS, 1991, 72 pages, softbound, $12.95

Missouri Heritage Quilts by Bettina Havig
#1718: AQS, 1986, 104 pages, softbound, $14.95

Nancy Crow: Quilts and Influences by Nancy Crow
#1981: AQS, 1990, 256 pages, hardcover, $29.95

No Dragons on My Quilt by Jean Ray Laury with
Ritva Laury and Lizabeth Laury
#2153: AQS, 1990, 52 pages, hardcover, $12.95

Oklahoma Heritage Quilts Oklahoma Quilt Heritage Project
#2032: AQS, 1990, 144 pages, softbound, $19.95

Scarlet Ribbons: American Indian Technique for Today's Quilters
by Helen Kelley
#1819: AQS, 1987, 104 pages, softbound, $15.95

Sets & Borders by Gwen Marston and Joe Cunningham
#1821: AQS, 1987, 104 pages, softbound, $14.95

Somewhere in Between: Quilts and Quilters of Illinois
by Rita Barrow Barber
#1790: AQS, 1986, 78 pages, softbound, $14.95

Stenciled Quilts for Christmas by Marie Monteith Sturmer
#2098: AQS, 1990, 104 pages, softbound, $14.95

Texas Quilts–Texas Treasures Texas Heritage Quilt Society
#1760: AQS, 1986, 160 pages, hardbound, $24.95

Treasury of Quilting Designs, A by Linda Goodmon Emery
#2029: AQS, 1990, 80 pages, 14 x 11, spiral-bound, $14.95

These books can be found in local bookstores and quilt shops. If you are unable to locate a title in your area, you can order by mail from AQS, P.O. Box 3290, Paducah, KY 42002-3290. Please add $1 for the first book and 40¢ for each additional one to cover postage and handling